Visiting Chernobyl

A Considered Guide for Travelers
What You'll See and What to Know

Also by Bill Murray

Common Sense and Whiskey:
Modest Adventures Far from Home

Visiting Chernobyl

A Considered Guide for Travelers
What You'll See and What to Know

Bill Murray

EP

EarthPhotos Books
Young Harris, Georgia USA • 2013

Visiting Chernobyl

A Considered Guide for Travelers
What You'll See and What to Know

Because of the dynamic nature of the internet, some of the web sites mentioned in this book may have changed or may no longer be valid.

Photographs in this book are available for purchase or download from, and appear on, the web site EarthPhotos.com.

Printed in the United States of America.

ISBN-13: 978- 0- 9910697-0-5
ISBN-10: 0991069706

Front Cover Photograph: The kindergarten in Kopachi village, Ukraine
Back Cover Photograph: The amusement park in Pripyat, Ukraine

Visit these associated web sites:
CommonSenseAndWhiskey.com
EarthPhotos.com

EarthPhotos Books
4625 Murray Lane
Young Harris, GA 30582 USA
www.earthphotos.com
800.229.2046
706.379.0675

•••••

Neophyte Publishing
2013

CONTENTS

•••••

INTRODUCTION

When Chernobyl's reactor 4 blew up Ukraine wasn't yet a country. It was an important republic in the Union of Soviet Socialist Republics. The capital of Ukraine was the U.S.S.R.'s third city after Moscow and St. Petersburg. Kiev was the capital of the Ukrainian Soviet Socialist Republic, and it was just over an hour away from Chernobyl.

Chernobyl was the worst nuclear accident in history. At first violent explosions of steam carried radiation downwind. An experiment gone wrong led to catastrophic power surges inside the reactor building. Ultimately the roof just blew away, a million pounds of concrete. Fire filled the sky. The reactor's graphite core, radioactive and deadly, burned like charcoal for ten days.

People called the defensive, secretive Soviet reaction to Chernobyl a catalyst for the young leader Mikhail Gorbachev's glasnost and perestroika. Some say the way Moscow handled it, and how that changed Soviet citizens' view of their government set in train the demise of the entire Soviet system.

Today, with minimal bureaucracy, you can visit Chernobyl to see things for yourself. The visit in this book took place in March 2013. It was arranged by Solo East Travel at tourkiev.com.

This is not a "how to visit Chernobyl" guide. Rather it's a short account of the types of things you're likely to see if you visit for a day. And it's just about the right length for you to read on the flight over. I hope you enjoy it.

Bill Murray, Young Harris, Georgia
October, 2013

1 KINDERGARTEN

The kindergarten at Kopachi

The fence fell over itself, a cascade of wooden slats. It was hard to tell with everything covered by snow, but probably the trees between here and the building grew up since the accident. Down the road radiation signs stuck out of long earthen mounds.

This was Kopachi village, not far inside the ten kilometer inner zone around Chernobyl. They buried Kopachi, almost the whole village. Maybe that was a good idea in desperate days, but burying things forced radioactive material toward the water table. So once they thought twice they stopped burying to think things through.

At first they'd bury villages whole, especially across the border in Belarus. They'd dig pits, push entire houses in and cover them up. Special trucks, who knows where they came from, sprayed water up and down the streets all the time, because all the dust that burying kicked up was radioactive.

Belarus buried more than a hundred villages. Conscripts sent down here by Minsk did it. They filled up all the wells they could find with concrete trying to protect ground water.

It's only ten miles (16 kilometers) from reactor 4 to Belarus, and on April 26th, 1986 the wind blew straight to the border. That meant between half and two thirds of all the radiation fell on

Belarusian farmers who lived on whatever produce they coaxed from the soil, and on the family livestock.

Authorities moved over a hundred thousand Belarusians in a hurry, to places with no housing and little employment. Twenty per cent of Belarus's agricultural land was rendered useless.

Ten years on, farmers could breed horses and cattle for beef but not for milk, and 32,000 square miles, the area of South Carolina, remained too radioactive to use. That's nearly a quarter of the country.

•••••

They commissioned studies and they anguished and eventually they worked out how to bury things more safely. They'd dig a pit and before they pushed anything in they'd line the bottom and sides with four feet of clay. Then they'd bury the bad stuff, seal up the top with clay and add soil and grass.

It was better than that mad bulldozing they did at first. One thing though, still today they have to keep trees off the mounds. Roots make the crypts leak.

The kindergarten at Kopachi

They left two buildings in Kopachi, I don't know why. Ice lurked up under the snow, you knew it, so you crept along step by step. Bum place to slip and get hauled out to Kyiv in the militia's ambulance up at the checkpoint.

You had to bat away tree branches to get up the walk to the kindergarten. Nobody here to chop them down. Rose bushes intruded as prickly hazards up the walk. There were no foot prints, so nobody had been here since the newly fallen snow, a day or two. Icicles hung from the window frames. No glass.

Igor held his dosimeter to the ground. 6.04 microSieverts per hour.

The kindergarten in Kopachi was a solid old thing, a brick building with four columns, fading blue paint around the wood of the windows. All over the floor papers were scattered about, workbooks with activities, kid stuff like coloring and matching similar objects.

Somebody had brought a little metal tricycle with a metal seat inside, its rubber tires gone. A spoon sat on a low table and a green poster board, I think a science project, was propped up against the wall behind it. You had to skirt a charred spot in the floor where somebody once set a fire.

A cabinet, a tea cup, a grown-up's coffee mug. A stuffed bear leaned back, propped against a chalkboard on the little tray where the chalk would be.

Kopachi Kindergarten Classroom

Three narrow wooden doors hung crooked, kind of defiant, open and upright. Cabinets listed down at the end of the hall. Somebody had spilled their insides out all over the floor, a pretty pointless thing to do. A bottle of glue sat alone on a shelf. A tree poked right through the window.

Down the corridor bunk beds filled up a whole room, cloth safety nets around the top bunks. The original 1986 covers and pillows. They must have been. Who'd smuggle in soiled blankets?

Paint peeled in palm-of-your-hand sized slices. A children's book was titled Barvinok. In Ukrainian that's 'periwinkle.'

The kindergarten

Two girl dolls, one in long johns, the other barefoot in a pinafore, lay on one bed's lower frame. Snow piled up on the trees. One window still had glass.

People had posed things for pictures: a book opened to a particular page on a window sill, gas masks on the floor. After 27 years this wasn't April 1986. People had been here. Workers brought in for the clean-up effort for example (they called them 'liquidators'), took whatever they needed wherever they found it. Families came back now and again to salvage what they could of their own things. And Kyiv let contracts to salvage scrap metal, resulting in ripped out window frames and pipes.

And the looting. Igor lamented "bad people," and he was so innocent, such a wide eyed academic, that you thought along with him, "Yeah, those bad, bad people." Igor had no guile. He always called it "OUR government" like a boy scout. He was utterly unaffected and you had to love him.

The government cracked down hard on the looting. You didn't want radioactive teddy bears finding their way to Kyiv after all, or hot batteries driving around in cars.

The kindergarten wasn't exactly a freeze frame of April 26th, 1986, but little girls' dolls, 80s style tricycles and rusted cribs in the school? They'll still get to you, 27 years on.

•••••

2 THE ROAD UP

Twenty five people and their guides visited the Chernobyl exclusion zone on a Saturday in March, 2013: Three Norwegian photographers, a bus with 18 including Germans, Hungarians, Austrians, and a Ukrainian woman and her American boyfriend. There was a Honda carrying two people that nobody ever saw again and then my wife and great traveling partner Mirja and me and our driver and guide, both named Igor.

•••••

In Kyiv, snow screamed out of the sky. The hotel had a pretty good view, up on a hill, and beyond the curtains the whole world was ivory. Minus six in the morning with a high of minus 3 promised. People clomped through town with their heads down, snow-grumpy. Should have been signs of spring by now, they groused, but all you got were big black stacks of snow on sidewalks and this chafing, bitter wind.

If you walked straight out the hotel door past St. Michael's Cathedral you could follow the traffic to Maidan Nezalezhnosti (Independence Square), a strange brew of postwar Stalinism and curious modern glass domes. It's grand enough for a main square but not presumptuous and surely not imposing. The wind whipped up and down it, and I couldn't imagine how they all managed to camp outside (in tents!) during the Orange Revolution, which ran between November and January eight years ago.

Protests against the jailing of former Prime Minister Yulia Tymoshenko (since October 2011) continued inside dirty, opaque tents. In the spirit of the revolution, I guess.

Maidan Square fills a sort of a well below St. Michael's down to the full-Stalinist Vul Kreschatyk, Kyiv's Champs-Élysées. Mirja judged it soulless.

Kyiv, Ukraine with Maidan Square lit in the center

Kreschatyk Street splays out needlessly wide in that intimidating communist way, though not as absurdly as Prospekt Nezavisimosti, a bigger boulevard in the smaller Belarusian capital of Minsk, Kyiv's dull and unhappy neighbor to the north. You'd expect to see terrace cafes on the sidewalks wrapped in plastic with portable heaters like in any big city but they're just not there. Alas, the world's luxury brands have taken a pass on Kyiv, too. McDonald's and a Gap and a Marks and Spencer, sure. The rest was homegrown.

Igor had the car parked up on the sidewalk. A small human being dressed in black, wearing an impressive round cap, when Igor stood alongside his cab he looked you squarely in the chest.

First thing on a Saturday morning we sat inside the car as he quietly handled the details, the payments, the passport checks. He checked our papers against his company's records as registered with the Chernobyl authorities up at the checkpoint.

"It makes no sense to go" if the information doesn't match, Igor said. We would be turned back, even if it was just a clerical error.

Igor drove a Chevrolet Lacetti, by GM Daewoo, a modest little four door sedan from South Korea. All of them were gray, and Kyiv's streets turned them black with slush.

He brought along Misha, one of his company's guides for the Norwegian photographers, not for us. Just getting a ride up. Misha didn't turn around when we climbed in. Didn't say hello. Didn't say a damn thing. Misha didn't turn out to be a malevolent guy. Rather he meant his brusqueness to camouflage his shyness.

Really, Ukrainians are cloistered. The only people they've hung out with for the last hundred years come from the same part of the world and look and speak just like they do. If the most exotic place you'll visit in your whole life might be, say, Odessa, you've grown up amid all the diversity of an Appalachian courthouse. You won't be deft with things foreign.

(Which doesn't explain the difference between Slavic unease with strangers and any number of naturally welcoming cultures, Arabia to the South Pacific. I guess there are other reticent cultures. Pashtun comes to mind.)

Most people grow up poor in Ukraine. With what money would you travel? Now and then big western companies carry out small-bore poaching raids on software engineers for back-office work because they come cheaper than in the west. Engineers in bad suits travel from Kyiv to the Donbass coal producing region and back. And that's about it.

So what are Misha and Igor supposed to do to hone their hospitality skills? And anyway, people have a right to their peculiarities. Much loved Ukrainian war reporter and clandestine liberal Vasily Grossman wrote:

"Human groupings have one main purpose: to assert everyone's right to be different, to be special, to think, feel and live in his or her own way. People join together in order to win or defend this right. But this is where a terrible, fateful error is born: the belief that these groupings in the name of a race, a God, a party or a State are the very purpose of life and not simply a means to an end. No! The only true and lasting meaning of the struggle for life lies in the individual, in his modest peculiarities and in his right to these peculiarities."

Our Misha, a hardly fledged man of twenty, hadn't much considered Vasily Grossman. But he had been to Ocean City, Maryland twice, and the first time he overstayed his visa. Loved it. Worked in a program that appears to place Ukrainian youth in restaurant jobs for cheap in the US for a few months, somehow as part of their education.

Igor and Misha were both thin, Igor compact and wiry, Misha lanky, taller. Each wore caps and jeans, dark down jackets, and carried an equally dark humor. While the date was March 16th, "This is normal for February weather," Igor tossed over the seat. He meant the snow assault that continued every second until we left Kyiv three days later.

Two hours for the ride up, maybe more maybe less. Igor waffled his hand. Kyiv looked content tucked under its Saturday morning snow blanket.

Here was a funicular, the “Theatre for Kids,” storefronts advertising “advocats.” There was a new bridge going up to carry cars and subway trains across the Dnieper River.

As we ran alongside it I declared how cold it would be working up there today. Misha studied the bridge. “I don’t see anyone on bridge.”

Right.

The Dnieper River at Kyiv

He finally cracked, though, when I asked for a Cyrillic lesson on the difference between the letters Y and I, the second and third letters in “Kyiv.” (“Kiev” is the Russian spelling. At independence, Ukraine began spelling it in Ukrainian.) I was puzzled that both letters seem to have the "i" sound kind of like "Keev." Somehow this revealed Misha's vibrant inner linguist, who insisted that they are very different letters, with "Y" having a much harder sound, and "I" pronounced much more softly.

That broke down the walls. Now came a torrent of tour guideism. The radiation we could expect today would be less than you'd get naturally on a New York to Kyiv flight, because the atmosphere protects us from natural cosmic rays, and at 30,000 feet the atmosphere is thinner. Airline crews have higher occupational rates of exposure to radiation than nuclear industry workers.

The accident happened on April 26, 1986, before Misha was born. Misha's whole village was relocated en masse in 1993, seven years after the accident. Being four years old in 1993, he remembers that. But why did it take seven years to relocate his village?

The Soviet Union, run from Moscow, drew a 30 kilometer circle around the reactor, called it the exclusion zone and evacuated everyone. After the Soviet collapse, once Ukraine was administered from Kyiv again, the Emergencies Ministry amended the circle to take into consideration the varying levels of actual contamination in Ukraine.

Out in the suburbs, Igor pointed. "That is Petrici village. They are working in Kyiv for sure," he said.

Snow fell like fury, and covered the next town, a proper little place called Dimar. All the houses put fences at the road and hid behind them. Igor kept snapping photos of the snowy road. Surely he'd driven in worse. From Dimar emerged a two lane road, and slower now, in steady traffic, we drove deeper into the forest and an ominousness cloaked in white.

The road up

•••••

3 POLISSIA

Polissia is Europe's largest wetland, a land of bogs, swamps and unbroken stands of birch and pine that blend right across borders, Poland to Belarus to Ukraine into Russia. It's the size of Colorado.

It's the deep backwoods of both Ukraine and Belarus. Signs warn of moose. Logging trucks ply the roads. In wintertime snowdrifts weigh on the fields.

Polischuky are traditional people. The *Ukrainian Weekly Online* says they "live off the land much as their ancestors did before the automobile. They heat their homes with wood, harvest oats and raise dairy cattle, supplement their diets by hunting deer and rabbit and moose, and in late summertime they gather wild mushrooms and cranberries in the marshes.

"The woodlanders of Polissia ... take pride in their self-sufficiency, their determination to overcome hardships, to keep up their humor, even in the dead of winter. They ... can recount vivid stories of their forefathers' resistance to the Nazis and the Soviets. While the International Atomic Energy Agency has tried to promote a stereotype of Chornobyl survivors as hypochondriacs wallowing in self-pity and 'radiophobia,' the Polishchuky are more likely to impress visitors with their gritty optimism and their community spirit. Traditionally, the residents of this area raise large families of five children or more."

This corner of Polissia is known as the Pripet Marshes, after the Pripyat River, which runs right alongside the Chernobyl complex and drains into the Dnieper River bound for Kyiv and ultimately the Black Sea. Flooding from snowmelt in the spring periodically reimmerses contaminated soil. They've built eleven miles of dikes and dams to try to keep the Pripyat and Dnieper rivers, and Kyiv's water supply, clean.

Mistletoe-draped red pines outnumber birch trees all the way up to Chernobyl. It used to be they didn't know things like this, but now they have studies and it turns out that pine trees don't cope with radiation as well as birch. Grains and beans absorb cesium-137 way faster than they thought, too. Over the border, in contaminated areas of Belarus the state farms grow crops that naturally absorb less radiation for humans. Crops that absorb more, they grow as fodder.

Polissia landscape

Belarus can't afford to let a fifth of its agricultural land lay fallow. If producing radiation-free milk is too costly to make a profit, they'll raise cows for their meat. If food is contaminated the radiation control people show farmers how to make it safer, by boiling it, or soaking it in salt water. For poor farmers, even if they find out their food is contaminated, there's not much alternative.

Some parts of Belarus are still as radioactive as the exclusion zone, patches here and there across the eastern part of the country. It's a quilt of go and no-go areas that, anymore, are increasingly ignored.

•••••

4 CHERNOBYL TOWN AND THE EXCLUSION ZONE

A marsh, then a river. Eighty kilometers to go.

"Chernobyl, that way"

The road split at a "Chernobyl, that way" sign and Igor swung left. Snow blew across flat, fallow fields. A Lada sat on the roadside - police radar. You wouldn't want to be the man who sat in that little car all day on a day like today. As it turned out, that cop, or a fiend like him, nailed us on the way back.

Ivankov, home to maybe 40,000, was the last real town. They brought part of the surge of refugees here on Kyiv city buses in the first days back in 1986.

We shot through a roundabout and pointed straight on to Chernobyl.

The 30 kilometer checkpoint

Misha's Norwegian cameramen waited at the checkpoint, stamping in the snow, impatient. On the way up they called Igor to see where the hell we were. Igor turned prim and pointed out that they knew very well that the road was icy and he couldn't drive any faster. Maybe that was why he took those pictures.

There's a village called Dytyatky where the southern checkpoint stands outside the 30 kilometer radius around reactor 4. Metal bars crossed both lanes and administration buildings stood on each side.

Everybody out of the cars.

Snow filled the skies. Misha left with his frozen Norwegians and we found our guide, another man named Igor. We stood in the snow. Those who smoked, smoked while guards sorted out the permits.

Igor the driver got new paperwork each time he drove up. Igor the scientist-guide had a permanent pass, a laminated one.

Chernobyl town

Chernobyl sits inside the 30 kilometer circle on the highway from Kyiv, so it's a natural to administer the exclusion zone. Chernobyl InterInform, the part of the Emergencies Ministry that runs the zone, works out of Chernobyl town. Since 2009 there's even a newspaper, the ChNPP News.

Chernobyl Interinform runs a hotel for officials, scientists, flotsam and jetsam. "This is a bad, bad, bad hotel," driver Igor burst out with the most passion he'd muster all day.

Inside they hand out a safety notice that reads in part, "If you received notice about radioactive contamination, go to the person in charge for the hotel, or your attendant in the exclusion zone. To protect your skin use sports clothes, overalls and boots. Take with you plastic cloak, jackets or raincoats.

"Get from person in charge means of personal protection put on your personal protective gear, leave the premises and go to a safe place shown by the Director of "Chernobylinterinform" Agency or by the person in charge of civil defense matters (Anti-radiation Shelter - room # 8 in administrative building in 1aB.KhmelnitsckogoStr. or in printing house of the agency, located in 9 Radyanska str., Chernobyl). Further follow recommendations from the civil defense headquarter."

You have to stay inside the hotel, which Igor declared permanently dismal, all the time unless you have an escort.

Chernobyl Interinform's Hotel Pripyat, Chernobyl town

Chernobyl Interinform runs a food hall, too. At the end of the tours they bring you, the drivers and guides for a hurried meal. Borscht, pelmeni, salads. Get 'em in, get 'em out.

Choosing Chernobyl to administer the zone meant people would be here all the time. Certain infrastructure had to be changed. They would no longer use the underground water pipes, radiation having seeped into the ground, and rather than disturb the irradiated soil, workers built a new system of pipes above and across the roads.

Welcome to Chernobyl

Some 7000 people work in the zone today, 3000 in research and administrative jobs (like Igor the scientist/guide), around 2700 associated with the power plant and about 1000 working on the French-led new sarcophagus construction.

Roughly a thousand more mostly elderly samosely, or "self-settlers" have moved back into the exclusion zone since 1986, about two hundred of whom remain, a few in Chernobyl town, the rest scattered across small villages.

Many workers live in Slavutych, a sputnik (satellite) city of around 25,000 built northeast of the zone after the accident. There are two main work schemes. Some people are on four days then off for four, and the rest work fifteen days straight and then get fifteen days off.

I thought having fifteen days off in a row amounted to a good job but driver Igor thought differently.

"Good job no. Good job is sitting in office. And banker is good job."

Our second Igor was first a scientist; tour-guiding was his second job. He was a Ukrainian bear of a man in a ushanka (literally "ear hat," one of those with flaps), a fur hat that he politely took off in the car. He was your older brother, beefy with bright blue eyes and an open, trustable face, a bit of a nerd in the scientist's way, which was lovable, actually. But he struggled with English. At first he was all facts and figures, plodding a bit, and somehow that was a little spooky, hearing about uprooted animals and people in a thick Slavic drone as we drove further into the zone, the world constricted by snow.

There is a monument at the fire station outside Chernobyl town. The Igors said it was for the firefighters and they thought it was erected by their families, or at any rate with private money.

Monument to the firefighters, Chernobyl

Six men fight fire in the monument. The Soviet press lionized six firemen who died fighting the immediate disaster. Two of them got the country's highest honorary title, Hero of the Soviet Union.

Outside Chernobyl town stood tiny horses. Creating the exclusion zone created a de facto nature reserve, and in 1998 and 1999 they introduced several dozen Przewalski's (pronounced "chevalski's") horses, an endangered species of wild horse native to the Central Asian steppes.

Left on their own, in less than ten years the Przewalski's herd grew from 21 to 64. At first they appeared to thrive, although in the last two years the herd size has declined from a high of 65 to just 30 or 40. In a BBC report a researcher at the

Przewalski's horses inside the exclusion zone

Ukrainian Academy of Science named Sergiy Paskevych said, “It is difficult to say what affect the lives of these animals. Maybe it’s the wolves ... or maybe it’s disease. Of course, the anthropogenic factor cannot be excluded.”

He meant poaching. Biologist Igor Chizhevsky, who has worked in the zone, said field workers have found horses that have had been shot dead, presumably by poachers.

Igor the scientist studied the animals, too. He twisted around in the front seat, all animated, and talked about the animals he loved, wolves, beavers, foxes, lynx, and rotten dogs, by which I expect he meant rabid, or wild.

Specifically, his own field of interest is the transfer of radionuclides from the soil to organisms, namely the predators and cattle and sheep here in the zone.

And right there in the first place, in definitions, he had me. Best I’ve learned, let’s just say that nuclides are a sort of species of atom grouped by atomic number, which is the number of protons found in the nucleus of an atom, and radionuclides are nuclides that are radioactive.

A whole radionuclide industry thrived here after 1986 and Igor personifies it now. He began in 1993, finding work on a big survey, inventorying the wildlife in the exclusion zone. Rough estimates, he said, was all they were, based on visual identification and extrapolations from the size of animals' territories.

"twice lower than safe normal"

He opened his little guide's satchel and produced a dosimeter. Just inside the exclusion zone gate it read 0.15 microSieverts per hour, which he said was "twice lower than safe normal."

•••••

5 RADIATION

For all the undoubted personal tragedy, the worst nuclear accident in history wasn't as bad as it might have been. Either a total core 'meltdown' in which uranium melted into the earth and poisoned groundwater, or winds from the north carrying radiation to Kyiv, would have increased thyroid cancer and leukemia deaths.

The core didn't melt down, it blew apart. What happened was, a series of violent steam explosions blew the roof off the reactor building, allowing radiation to escape downwind.

An experiment gone awry in the early hours of April 26th, 1986, led to catastrophic power surges inside the reactor building. Intense heat combined with cooling water blew the roof off the building, exposing the graphite core inside the reactor to air. Further explosions shattered the core, showering radioactive graphite through the open countryside and further radiation into the air.

To thoroughly understand what happened requires the recondite knowledge of a physicist, but the basic concepts are easy enough.

When an atom splits apart it's called fission. Nuclear reactors facilitate fission; they split atoms. In Chernobyl's case, uranium atoms.

One reason there is a nuclear power industry at all is how much better fission produces energy than burning coal. The energy released by fission in one gram of uranium is the equivalent of burning three tons of coal.

Uranium emits high energy neutrons, which are bits of the nucleus of an atom. When one of these particles collides with another uranium atom just so, it forces a particle out of that atom. That's "splitting" an atom. If the same thing happens again and again all of these particles flying around release energy in the form of heat. The reactor uses the heat to boil water, generate steam and turn turbines to produce electricity. It's the same thing coal plants do with the heat they get from burning coal.

Not so exotic after all, and simple enough. But a couple of things are vital in managing the release of heat from fission:

Uranium particles fly around so fast that they're likely to fly off into space and never collide with another uranium particle. If you want them to collide, you need to slow them down.

What might help slow them down? Water, for one thing. But graphite, a mineral, works too, and so at Chernobyl they built a seven meter (23 foot) high block of graphite with long holes inside for the uranium. The big graphite column is called the reactor core.

The idea was to keep the uranium rods down in the core and thus 'moderated,' or slowed by the graphite, causing neutrons to collide with uranium atoms more than they would otherwise. That would release still more particles and thus, additional energy.

The more energy, the hotter the reactor would get, so you'd want to control the reactions inside the core to keep the reactor from overheating. It turns out the chemical element boron absorbs the particles thrown off by uranium, so at Chernobyl there were holes for boron rods as well as holes for uranium roads in the graphite core. They call the boron rods "control rods."

Inserting or withdrawing the control rods from the core could control the rate of the reaction, or stop it altogether. To produce more heat they would lift the control rods out of the core so they would absorb fewer particles. To cool things off, they'd lower the control rods into the core so they'd absorb more.

By design there were 211 control rods in reactor 4. If all of them were lowered into the reactor core the boron would absorb enough uranium particles to stop the reaction completely. Just shut it down.

The trouble at Chernobyl was, when the critical moment arrived a series of human errors and a design flaw in the control rods combined to prevent the rods from getting into the core.

If there were ever a problem in the reactor it would be crucial for the electricity-producing turbines to continue to produce enough electricity for emergency operations, to work the cooling pumps and control rods, emergency lighting for the control room and control panel, things like that.

The design of the reactor required twenty seconds to position the control rods in an emergency, so it was imperative that the turbines continue to produce electricity for at least those twenty seconds. That's what they were testing on the night of the accident. It's something they should have done before the reactor ever opened for business.

Have you ever left a critical ingredient out of a recipe and ruined the dish? That's what Chernobyl's designers and engineers did. Except they cooked themselves.

●●●●●

6 SHUT DOWN THE REACTOR!

The clocks stopped in reactor 4 at 1:23 Saturday morning. The whole idea of what happened was so shocking, so enormous that it took until the sun came up for Aleksandr Akimov, the reactor 4 shift chief, to come to grips with the facts and by then he was far along toward dying. In the first light of day he and everyone else saw that 500 tons of roof had blown off reactor 4. The graphite that once moderated the uranium fuel lay in smoldering bits on the ground.

That kind of evidence was hard to deny.

The experiment was originally scheduled for the day before, Friday. To conduct the experiment reactor 4 had to be brought down to a fraction of its normal power output. When they started to reduce the output in accordance with the plan, about 14:00 the load dispatcher down in Kyiv called to say he needed that power, so the experiment moved to the overnight shift, which started at midnight.

Whether that led to the accident and sealed the fate of the reactor, people hash and rehash that still. Some argue that the delay helped cause the accident because it replaced the veteran day shift senior engineer with a 26 year old night shift operator named Leonid Toptunov.

There is no question that postponing the experiment kept casualties down. Two thousand people worked on the under-construction reactors 5 and 6 during the day, and lots fewer people were outside at 1:00 a.m. than would have been in the middle of a pretty spring afternoon.

Grigoriy Medvedev, a nuclear engineer who wrote the first detailed account of the accident, placed blame with Anatoli S. Dyatlov, the deputy chief engineer for operations and test supervisor. He described Dyatlov as "lean, with a smoothly combed dull-gray head of hair and evasive, deep-set, and lustreless eyes," who "did not know nuclear technology" and "clearly did not have experience in human relations."

Others designed the experiment, but Dyatlov, as supervisor, changed the plans. He decided to turn off the emergency cooling system, which would flood the reactor with water if ever it became too hot. Dyatlov apparently thought that by turning off the water he was protecting the reactor from heat shock if cold water should hit it.

He probably felt confident he had a fail safe in any emergency. By the plant's very design, the entire nuclear reaction could be shut down by lowering the control rods into the graphite core. Except it didn't turn out to be quite that simple.

Dyatlov didn't just turn the cooling system off, making 350 cubic meters of emergency water unavailable to cool the reaction once it went out of control. He also had the pipes' valves physically closed and padlocked so that they couldn't even be opened by hand.

The experiment required disabling a sort of autopilot, a system that monitored conditions inside the reactor and raised and lowered the control rods as necessary to maintain performance.

When the time came to do that Leonid Toptunov, the kid night shift reactor engineer, flipped the switch and just about had a heart attack. He watched the power drop precipitously, from 1500 to just 30 megawatts. That ruined the experiment in the first place because such low power poisons a reactor with products of radioactive decay like iodine and xenon which, like boron in the control rods, act to slow the nuclear reaction.

In *Chernobyl Notebook*, Grigoriy Medvedev writes, "The reactor was being poisoned, the power either had to be raised immediately or wait a day for the poisoning to be dispelled...."

Dyatlov intimidated Toptunov and upbraided the whole crew. Medvedev wrote, "He raged around, he rushed around the unit control room, and he wasted valuable minutes." He wanted the experiment to proceed.

Toptunov began to pull out control rods, trying to raise the power. He pulled out rod after rod, but the plant's design specs required at least 30 (of the 211) control rods to stay in the reactor at all times.

At 30 rods, Toptunov defied Dyatlov. He would not take out any more. Night shift supervisor Aleksandr Akimov backed him up.

Dyatlov pressured the crew. He called Akimov "a lying idiot."

To Toptunov, "What are you yapping about, you oaf?"

"If you do not take it back up, Tregub will do it...."

Tregub was Yuri Tregub, Akimov's counterpart on the previous shift. Akimov relieved Tregub at midnight and Tregub, who should have conducted the experiment the afternoon before, had stayed to watch.

Toptunov folded. He took out all but eighteen control rods in reactor 4. *

Again, Medvedev: "(T)he reactor's capacity for excursion now exceeded the ability of the available safety systems to shut down the device. And still it was decided to continue the tests."

Dyatlov thought they could shut down the reactor by lowering all the control rods, but it was already too late.

* According to Toptunov's testimony before he died, as told by Grigoriy Medvedev. The Soviet report to the IAEA said there were eleven rods. Marianne Barisonek in *Cause and Effect: Understanding Chernobyl* writes that there were only six.

The reactor was so hot the cooling water normally inside the reactor boiled away into steam. Pressure built inside the reactor.

There was a button on the control panel at reactor 4, in effect a panic button, called the AZ-5, which would initiate the reactor's emergency protection system and insert all the control rods.

Here is the same story two ways. Marianne Barisonek writes in *Cause and Effect: Understanding Chernobyl*:

"Toptunov shouted that the reactor power had reached an emergency stage. Akimov shouted back, 'Shut down the reactor!' He dashed to the control desk and hit the button...."

As Grigoriy Medvedev has it:

"... Leonid Tuptonov first sounded the alarm. 'The emergency safety needs to be activated, Aleksandr

Fedorovich, we have an excursion,' he told Akimov.... 'I am pressing the emergency safety!' Akimov shouted and reached for the red button."

And now a basic, maddening and inexplicable flaw in the design of this particular reactor came into play. The core was seven meters (23 feet) tall, and so were the control rods, but the absorbent boron rods had a meter of hollow space on either end.

It's a bloody emergency! Forget the rule book! Shove the control rods in there right now!

As the meter-long hollow tips of the rods entered the graphite core (193 of them, all at once!), before the boron could reach the core and begin to shut down the nuclear reaction the rods displaced much of the rest of the cooling water in the core, causing more steam and speeding up the reaction rather than shutting it down. The power of the reactor surged beyond 100 per cent in a fraction of a second, before the boron reached the core.

At once Akimov saw from the control panel that the rods moved only two or two and a half meters instead of the full seven, then stopped.

Dull thumps came from the central hall. Everybody heard them. Akimov rushed to release the clutch on the motors so the rods would drop into the core of their own weight. They didn't move.

A worker in the turbine room heard a low boom.

The core baked and fractured, warping the channels that should guide the control rods into the core. There was nothing to stop the reaction.

The roof blew off the building and bits of graphite were ultimately found as far away as Poland. Remnants of the graphite core burned for ten days. Toptunov died at the clinic designated to handle radiation cases in Moscow. He said, "I might cause a power surge but if I don't do what I'm told, I'll be fired."

7 THE SCRAMBLE TO RESPOND

Two minutes after the explosion the fire station alarm rang. The firefighters who scrambled from sleep to the scene, along with the regular overnight shift at reactor 4, were among the first fatally irradiated. They were unquestioned heroes, battling the blazes until dawn with no special training for a nuclear accident, in shirtsleeves, using only conventional firefighting methods. They walked amid flaming, radioactive graphite.

The power station fire brigade arrived first. Lieutenant Volodymyr Pravik, their commander, could see right away he needed help and called in fire brigades from Pripyat and Chernobyl.

When Pravik died thirteen days later he was a month shy of age 24. This is what his doctor in Moscow said, as quoted on *The Chernobyl Project* website:

"The radiation came to affect his salivary glands; his mouth went dry like a desert and thus Pravik was unable to speak any more. He could only stare with those expressive eyes, blinking bare eyelids, refusing to submit to death. Then his internal resistance forces began to weaken and gradually dry up. Pravik began to die. The loss of flesh from his eyes. He began to melt. Dry. Fade. This mummified skin and irradiated tissue. For each hour, for each day, this human being ceased - ceased, ceased, ceased! Damn this nuclear age! It's not even possible to die in a human way. Deceased - blackened, withered mummy..."

•••••

The Finns have a term for naïveté. They call it being "blue-eyed." It's hard for me to believe after-the-fact accounts of reactor employees and first responders being blue-eyed, unaware of the dangers. Chernobyl was a nuclear plant generating power from nuclear fission.
Which doesn't make their fates any less dire.

"We arrived there at 10 or 15 minutes to two in the morning," said fire engine driver Grigorii Khmal.

"We saw graphite scattered about. Misha asked: Is that graphite? I kicked it away. But one of the fighters on the other truck picked it up. It's hot, he said. The pieces of graphite were of different sizes, some big, some small, enough to pick them up...

"We didn't know much about radiation. Even those who worked there had no idea. There was no water left in the trucks. Misha filled a cistern and we aimed the water at the top. Then those boys who died went up to the roof – Vashchik, Kolya and others, and Volodya Pravik.... They went up the ladder ... and I never saw them again."

Another fireman told the BBC, "It was dark because it was night. On the other hand, you could see and even recognize a person from 10 to 15 meters. It was if (sic) the sun was rising, but with a strange light."

They climbed to the roof of what was left of reactor 4, preventing fire from spreading to the other three reactors and so preventing what could have been a truly ghastly night. By 5:00 a.m. all the fires were out save for the one in the reactor. That's the fire that burned for ten days. It took 5000 tons of sand, boron, dolomite and clay dropped from helicopters to put it out. Five thousand tons. Four helicopter crewmen died when a helicopter clipped a wire and crashed while dropping clay onto the reactor.

•••••

The political heart of the U.S.S.R. was aware of the accident within an hour and a half. V. V. Maryin, the head of the nuclear power sector of the CPSU Central Committee got a call at three o'clock in the morning.

His wife Alfa Fedorovna Martynova told Grigoriy Medvedev, "On 26 April 1986 at 0300 hours, the intercity phone rang in our house. Bryukhanov was calling Maryin from Chernobyl. When he finished the conversation, Maryin told me: 'A horrible accident at Chernobyl; but the reactor is intact....' He quickly dressed and called for his car. Just before he left, he called the highest leadership of the party's central committee up through channels. First of all, Frolyshev. He in turn called Dolgikh. Dolgikh called Gorbachev and the members of the politburo."

They reacted fast operationally, dispatching teams to the scene, but the leadership remained outwardly opaque for days. When Sweden raised the alarm two days later, the rest of the world began asking questions, forcing the Politburo into an emergency meeting.

What to divulge?

As little as possible, they decided. The evening of the day they evacuated Pripyat, the 28th, they read this on Vremya, the nightly TV newscast:

"An accident has taken place at the Chernobyl power station, and one of its reactors was damaged. Measures are being taken to eliminate the consequences of the accident. Those affected by it are being given assistance. A government commission has been set up."

Censors in Moscow assured nothing more was reported. And here is the irretrievable breach of trust, the crime the regime could never put right: Putting its reputation before its citizens' health.

Because for the two days between the accident and the announcement on Vremya, while local officials remained silent, fire raged in the blown open reactor 4. And families across Pripyat, after a winter pent up in apartment blocks, basked unaware in the warm spring sunshine.

•••••

Western Europe worked itself into a great frenzy. Three hours after the first Soviet report a Dutch nuclear research lab suggested there had been a complete meltdown of one of the reactors.

By Tuesday morning photos from an American satellite shocked analysts, who saw the roof blown off reactor 4 and the inside still glowing. That same day the Polish government decided to hand out iodine tablets to children on their border near Ukraine.

Scientists jumped on the case with a vengeance. They tested people arriving from Kyiv and found that those arriving before May 1st brought no radiation on their skin, hair and clothing but those who were in Kyiv from May 1st on, did. They determined what types of radionuclides were released and decided those would only be released at temperatures indicating that the reactor core had at least partially melted.
For weeks Europeans drank powdered milk and scrubbed their vegetables. Some places banned fresh produce and milk.

Twenty-five years on we follow catastrophes anywhere in the world in real time, so it's hard to remember the closed nature of the Soviet system in Gorbachev's early days (He was just thirteen months into the job of General Secretary when the accident happened). With complicit local leaders, they kept word of the accident from Kiev, just 90 kilometers (55 miles) away, and Minsk, about 350 kilometers (215 miles) away, long enough for the annual May 1st May Day parades to be held on open, radioactive streets five full days later, three days after the ten kilometer circle around reactor 4 was evacuated. Apparently that was to make everything appear under control.

The day after the parade, May 2nd, the 30 kilometer zone was designated for evacuation. On May 6th, after eleven days, they closed the schools in Kyiv and the radio urged everyone to stay indoors and not to eat leafy greens. It took eighteen days for Gorbachev to go on TV with his own account of the disaster.

•••••

8 MEDICAL CALAMITY

No one believes the official Soviet count of 31 deaths directly attributed to the accident but no one agrees what the number should be, either. Twenty eight of the thirty one were firefighters who died within months. One hundred thirty four developed acute radiation sickness. A United Nations report estimates 4,000 excess cancer deaths; other estimates range much higher.

There is a big, imposing old building at number 26 Novaya Basmanaya Street northeast of the Kremlin in Moscow. Clinic number six specialized in radiation and nuclear issues, and from the start it was nearly overcome with patients, because while political Moscow showed itself ham-handed, the medical establishment proved adroit. By nightfall on the first day, only sixteen-odd hours after the blast, they'd flown 129 patients into clinic number six. 170 more followed the next day.

Specialized first responders flew to Chernobyl in half a day. Medical units gathered in Moscow scant hours after the accident, before dawn, and arrived in Kiev at 11:00 a.m. They examined over a thousand people.

Ultimately 5000 doctors and nurses descended on Polissia, especially therapeutic radiologists and hematologists. In Moscow some 300 more provided care. Forty-year studies are ongoing to compare cancer rates of evacuees to control groups. It's the largest study since Hiroshima.

The reactor 4 night crew supervisor, thirty-three year old Aleksandr Akimov, died from radiation poisoning in clinic number six after two weeks. To the end he remained defiant and in denial. He thought he'd done everything right.

His wife told Grigoriy Medvedev, "While he could still talk, he kept repeating to his father and mother that he had done everything right. This tortured him to the very end. He also said that he had no complaints to make against the personnel of his shift. They had done their duty.

"I visited my husband the day before he died. At that point, he could no longer speak. But there was pain in his eyes. I knew he was thinking about that damned night, he was reenacting everything inside himself over and over again and he could not see that he was to blame. He received a dose of 1,500 roentgens, perhaps even more, and he was doomed. He became blacker and blacker, and on the day he died he was as black as a Negro. He was charred all over. He died with his eyes open...."

They called this the "nuclear tan." From the inside out.

Vyacheslav Stepanovych Brazhnik, senior turbine machinist, stayed in the turbine hall when the building exploded, trying to stabilize things. He too received a fatal dose. According to Medvedev: "Brazhnik lay there all swollen, dark brown. He strained to say that his whole body pained terribly and that he was weak....

"He was in a very bad way, and I did not want to ask him any more questions. He was constantly asking for something to drink. I would give him Borzhomi mineral water.

"The pain, pain, everywhere.... The pain could be so terrible...."

They awarded Brazhnik the order "for courage."

Viktor Vasilyevich Proskuryakov was a trainee and recipient of the same posthumous award. When Akimov began to realize the scale of the disaster that night, he implored Proskuryakov to go into the reactor building and fix it by hand. Akimov sent him to his death, with 100% radiation burns.

Grigoriy Medvedev:

"I went to see Proskuryakov 2 days before he died. He was lying on an inclined bed. His mouth was horribly swollen. No skin on his face. Bare. Bandages on his chest. Heat lamps above him. He asked constantly for something to drink. I had mango juice with me. I asked if he wanted some juice. He said that he did, very much. He was tired,he said, of the mineral water. A bottle of Borzhomi stood on his bedside table. I helped him to drink the juice from a glass...."

"The SIUR (reactor operator) Lenya Toptunov had his father on watch by the bedside. He had already given his bone marrow for his son's transplant. But it did not help. He stayed at his son's bedside day and night, he would turn him over. He was burned to blackness all over. Only his back was still light-colored...."

•••••

Armand Hammer, the American chairman of Occidental Petroleum who made a second career as interlocutor with the Soviets, arranged a team of U.S. doctors bearing American medical equipment. Dr. Richard Champlin, chief of bone marrow transplant surgery at UCLA Medical Center, witnessed how doctors had to cope with "a critical shortage of technology and with equipment that dates back 20 years or more." Champlin found the old clinic in disrepair, with no air conditioning, overmatched and under-equipped for massive triage. The thing was, and may still be, that the Soviets bought most of their specialized hospital equipment from the United States and other western countries and manufactured very little themselves. Instead of determining blood counts in 20 seconds with an automated blood cell counter, for example, the Soviets counted blood cells under a microscope. That took thirty minutes they just didn't have.

Chernobyl bedeviled Moscow to the bitter end, right up to burying the victims' bodies. A. M. Khodakovsky, the man in charge of burying the dead, said "When it learned that the bodies were radioactive, the public health station demanded that concrete rafts be made at the bottom of the graves, as underneath the nuclear reactor, so that the radioactive fluids from the corpses would not go off into the groundwater. This was impossible, blasphemous, we argued with them for a long time. Finally, we agreed that the highly radioactive corpses would be soldered into zinc caskets. That is what we did."

They were laid into the earth in two rows in a "special area" of Mitinskoye Cemetery. Headstones of white marble recorded their names, dates of birth and death. Nothing more.

•••••

9 RULES AND STATISTICS

Igor recited his scientist statistics. He was good at data. He nailed all manner of facts just like you'd expect from a scientist, in the by-rote tone that lecturers use. He spoke of the firefighters poisoned from fighting the blaze, Pravik and Khmal and the rest who stood up in the open air on ladders above the ruined reactor with no radiation protection, in the middle of the night pouring water on a fire burning at 3600 degrees (2000 celsius) and taking in fatal doses of cesium 137, iodine 131, strontium 90 and other deadly radionuclides.

Igor took dosimeter readings all day. As we drove nearer the reactor we registered 2.4 microSieverts per hour. Not alarming. Not alarming at all. Lower than it might be "because we stay in car, plus snow is some protection" from the ground. The ground is bad. It's the main point of contamination because dust settles, and radiation with it.

They publish rules for visitors. For one thing, you must put nothing on the ground or on surfaces while in the exclusion zone, and they mean it. Igor held my camera while I dug into my shoulder bag to change the battery, rather than have me put the camera or the bag on a table, for example.

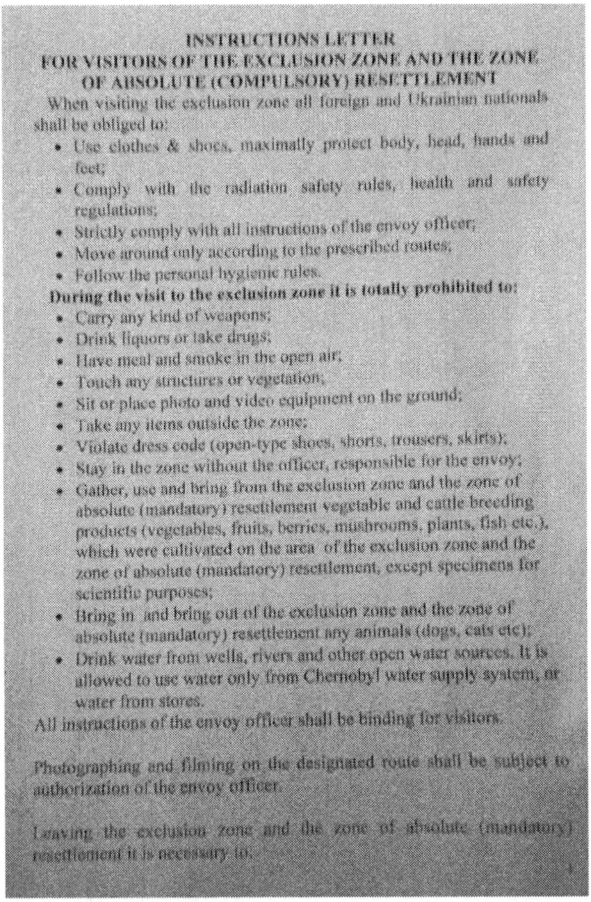

INSTRUCTIONS LETTER
FOR VISITORS OF THE EXCLUSION ZONE AND THE ZONE OF ABSOLUTE (COMPULSORY) RESETTLEMENT

When visiting the exclusion zone all foreign and Ukrainian nationals shall be obliged to:

- Use clothes & shoes, maximally protect body, head, hands and feet;
- Comply with the radiation safety rules, health and safety regulations;
- Strictly comply with all instructions of the envoy officer;
- Move around only according to the prescribed routes;
- Follow the personal hygienic rules.

During the visit to the exclusion zone it is totally prohibited to:

- Carry any kind of weapons;
- Drink liquors or take drugs;
- Have meal and smoke in the open air;
- Touch any structures or vegetation;
- Sit or place photo and video equipment on the ground;
- Take any items outside the zone;
- Violate dress code (open-type shoes, shorts, trousers, skirts);
- Stay in the zone without the officer, responsible for the envoy;
- Gather, use and bring from the exclusion zone and the zone of absolute (mandatory) resettlement vegetable and cattle breeding products (vegetables, fruits, berries, mushrooms, plants, fish etc.), which were cultivated on the area of the exclusion zone and the zone of absolute (mandatory) resettlement, except specimens for scientific purposes;
- Bring in and bring out of the exclusion zone and the zone of absolute (mandatory) resettlement any animals (dogs, cats etc);
- Drink water from wells, rivers and other open water sources. It is allowed to use water only from Chernobyl water supply system, or water from stores.

All instructions of the envoy officer shall be binding for visitors.

Photographing and filming on the designated route shall be subject to authorization of the envoy officer.

Leaving the exclusion zone and the zone of absolute (mandatory) resettlement it is necessary to:

1

You must also wear clothing with maximal protection for your body, head, hands and feet, and these, among several other things, are prohibited:

- eating or smoking in the open air
- touching vegetation
- wearing open-type shoes, shorts, skirts
- drinking water from wells, rivers and other open water sources

You sign and return the instruction letter. It tells you that "Possible irradiation dose is up to 3 microSv, which does not exceed the dose limit of population."

At a certain spot in the amusement park Igor knelt to hold the dosimiter near the ground because he knew the radiation was always high there. He was right. Igor's little patch, between the bumper cars and the ferris wheel, registered 8.65 microSieverts per hour.

How much is that? Well, standing on this spot for about twelve hours would give you a statistically increased risk of cancer. At 8.65 microSieverts you'd accumulate a lethal dose of radiation in about five weeks.

A lethal dose in five weeks

●●●●●

10 LIFE IN THE DEAD ZONE

You needn't leave the car at the Leliv checkpoint, on the ten kilometer inner circle around reactor 4. There's just a barrier across the road, lifted by guards. They call the ten kilometer zone the "dead zone," but take a look around. Everywhere you look, the only thing dead here is human activity.

In spite of the radiation, the Chernobyl exclusion zone is one of Europe's most vibrant and alive (and largest) nature reserves. Nobody has been here for 27 years, and nature has grown wild. Trees grow right up through buildings. Wildlife is unafraid.

The snow gave Pripyat's entire abandoned block after abandoned city block an other-worldly patina, a sense that this is no longer a place for man. But animals! Besides Igor's wolves, elk and rotten dogs, a Ukrainian ecologist named Serhiy Shaparenko says "such dispersed animal species as hare, fox, moose breed freely, and such rare for

Europe species as bear, lynx, badger and even Przevalsky's horse have found perfect shelter in the alienation zone."

Shaparenko thinks that "radiation impact is less harmful than human activities." Petr Kudan, director of the Polessky State Radio-Ecological Nature Reserve in Belarus, thinks so too. "Human interference is minimal, and we have a possibility to observe the evolution of wild nature. After the removal of anthropogenic stress, wildlife has recovered. Moreover, we specially imported some new species, including bison."

Reporters file lurid articles about eight-foot catfish in the cooling ponds around the reactor, but it turns out that's nothing to do with radiation. They're eight feet long because catfish grow all their lives. Once humans stopped catching them they grew too big for their other natural predators, raptors, to lift them out of the cooling ponds.

Remarkably, the reactor 4 building itself harbors life. A scientist named Sergey Gaschak told the

BBC, "A lot of birds are nesting inside the sarcophagus. Starlings, pigeons, swallows, redstart - I saw nests, and I found eggs."

Something else lurks inside reactor 4. A previously unknown and radical fungus flourishes, and it is probably not nature the wholesome and benign.

Inside the tomb, right alongside 200 tons of melted radioactive fuel, this particular fungus (a collection of more than one type, actually) uses gamma radiation as an energy source. In effect, it eats radiation to grow.

Robots found this black slime coating the reactor's walls. They returned samples of dark fungi rich in melanin, no different chemically than the substance that colors our skin. People knew there was melanin in fungi but nobody thought much about its biological role.

A radiology professor at the Albert Einstein College of Medicine in New York named Ekaterina Dadachova conducted tests that suggested that

“Just as the pigment chlorophyll converts sunlight into chemical energy that allows green plants to live and grow ... melanin can use a different part of the electromagnetic spectrum - ionizing radiation - to benefit the fungi containing it.”

Which sets up interesting avenues for research. If melanin in fungi turns radiation into food, could humans be getting part of their energy from radiation? Could organisms be living in the emptiness of space, where radiation is all around?

Today humans find fungi useful in decomposing organic matter, from food (mushrooms, yeasts, fermentation), to pesticides, to the production of antibiotics and detergents.

Maybe future human space explorers could eat radiation. The Einstein College researchers speculate that “Since ionizing radiation is prevalent in outer space, astronauts might be able to rely on fungi as an inexhaustible food source on long missions or for colonizing other planets.”

After 25 years Chernobyl teaches us all sorts of new lessons. Ben Lovejoy, in his fine blog, writes, “wildlife levels are not only back to pre-accident levels, but beyond. The habitat is now theirs alone. Environmentalists may talk of the risks posed to nature by man-made disasters, but the evidence from Prypiat is that nature does just fine, thanks - it's only the humans who have to worry.”

•••••

11 PRIPYAT AND THE REAL SOVIET UNION

Pripyat puts the face on Chernobyl because it's the place where real people lived. Besides the sarcophagus around reactor 4, the ferris wheel is the biggest icon of the place, and from the United States we squint at pictures of it like it's straight out of a horror movie. I've always looked around the edges of pictures of that little playground because somewhere out there, evil must lurk.

"What's that tower behind those trees?" I'd think. Part of something evil and nuclear, no doubt.

But Pripyat is a real place. You can stand on the town square and you can walk around and there are trees and buildings and air and nothing that's coming to get you. It's not evil and it doesn't feel evil.

Blame a closed, rights-denying state if you like but ultimately Chernobyl came from mankind's aspiring. Humans are fallible and an event like this would surely happen somewhere, sometime, a marker on the road of human progress. April 26th, 1986 brought hell to Chernobyl. Nearly thirty years on it's scary but it is not sinister; it's woeful but it is not wicked.

On the day hell came to Chernobyl reactor 5's cooling tower was done and the reactor itself had sprung up through a nest of cranes. The basement of reactor 6 was already dug. If all twelve reactors had come online the Chernobyl complex would have generated more electricity than anywhere else in the world.

You can't stand in the reactor complex without appreciating what Moscow meant to do. With four 1000-megawatt reactors online, reactors 5 and 6 under construction and ultimately twelve reactors envisioned, the Soviet Union set out to manhandle physics. As we all learned, forty-four years of human experience with nuclear power at the time proved insufficient to force nature to Soviet heel. But nobody knew it then.

That audacity was just the way the Soviets did things. They'd plan a model city for research and then they would build it. In the 1950's the Soviet Academy of Sciences built a city of 65,000 called Akademgorodok near Novosibirsk. With its three dozen institutes and academies and a huge library (that included foreign publications), it was a privilege to live in Akademgorodok, like it would be in Pripyat. Novosibirsk, 2800 kilometers (1750 miles) east of Moscow in Siberia, had a proper opera house.

Pripyat would be such a model city, by 1988 a sight to behold, clean, modern and full of amenities, a great place to raise kids. So full of scientists, bright young people with aspirations and future prospects that fifteen kindergartens were opened or planned.

Igor the scientist: "Average age was about 26 years old. Many peoples dream to live here and work at

Chernobyl power plant because salary was too much ... it was good job. And plus here was very good supply for food, for other product, for example."

They say that before the supermarket on Lenin Street stood looted, you could buy Chanel #5 there. I visited St. Petersburg after the Chernobyl accident and I can testify that you'd have been hard pressed to find imported perfume anywhere except the hard currency Berioska stores, because outside the little bubble where Pripyat and Chernobyl grew and thrived, the Soviet Union - all eleven time zones - was falling apart.

People in St. Petersburg, the Soviet Union's once elegant second city, went out with "just in case" bags to carry whatever they might chance to buy and, if they saw a queue in front of a store, they went to stand in it. In 1991 I never saw my friend Volodya without his just-in-case bag. The main Gastronom on Nevsky Prospeckt sold five things:

milk, cheese, bread, beer, and sausage. And there were maybe a hundred people in the sausage queue. About then the International Labor Organization said that "The Russian economy and the living standards of the Russian population have suffered the worst peacetime setbacks in any industrialised nation in history."

(That was shortly after the coup attempt when Boris Yeltsin stood on the tank outside the White House in Moscow. In *Down with Big Brother*, Michael Dobbs calls Yeltsin's first visit to an American supermarket - in Houston, in September, 1989 - a "turning point" on Yeltsin's road to populism and away from the U.S.S.R. The range of goods available to Americans without standing in line was beyond his imagination, far more impressive than U.S. icons like the Statue of Liberty.)

A week after I got home to Atlanta the November 21, 1991 New York Times wrote, "In another indication of Soviet food shortages, Anatoly Sobchak, the mayor of St. Petersburg, announced today that all types of food would be rationed beginning on December 15 because the city has been receiving only half the food it needs...."

There was real misery in Russia just then, political chaos, empty shelves, a plummeting currency, a loss of dignity. For comparison, at the time of the Chernobyl accident in 1986, a ruble cost a government-mandated $1.60. Five years later the official rate was 47 rubles for every dollar and nobody used the official rate.

But even at the official rate, otherwise perfectly respectable women, doctors, lawyers, might sneak out to the Astoria, St. Petersburg's dollar hotel, one night a month to earn $100 in an hour, 4700 rubles officially, where pensioners made 300 for a month.

•••••

That came later. In 1986 Pripyat was Disney World. It had movie theaters. There was child care. Three indoor swimming pools. An art school. Things were literally coming up roses.

"Many roses! This was city of roses. Government transplanted here fifteen thousand roses," Igor the driver, as it turned out another man for statistics, said.

Igor the scientist offered a wry smile: "But now only wild rose."

In 1986 Pripyat was on the march, its almost 49,000 people expected to eventually run up to 78,000, the size of Canton, Ohio. Pripyat's population zoomed past Chernobyl, which was home to just 14,000. Chernobyl was just a village, really, and Pripyat would be a new, proper city rising to support the power plant. Now Chernobyl is some kind of civic mutant, and Pripyat is nothing at all.

Buildings in Pripyat

Buildings in Pripyat

12 TO THE REACTOR

Snow swirled in every direction and as far as I knew we were lost, just driving around when out of the fog loomed the reactor 5 cooling tower. Cranes hung on each side of the reactor building that haven't moved since 1986. We turned along a wide boulevard.

Tough, heavy industrial park sounds rumbled and clanked across the road, muted by the snow. They came from the Novarka Batching Plant, a concrete factory serving the new sarcophagus that will cover reactor 4.

A fox charged the shoulder of the road, chest out, solitary and glowering. He stopped and stood his ground. Everybody glared back and forth until at length he walked away behind the rise. We could see he was eating but we couldn't see what he had killed.

The route to reactor 4 was restricted for security, and photos were sanctioned only from the one point that, now that you think about it, is what you see in all the photos. Driver Igor cautioned that we leave the windows up, no photos. He wanted to be clear that this wasn't a Ukrainian thing, that all countries maintain security at their nuclear sites.

The indignant fox

He hadn't had this experience, he said, but guides told stories of visitors spotted taking photos as they drove around the secure side of the reactor being stopped by militia with Kalashnikovs and detained for the rest of the day. The authorities asked non-contextual questions like "Who is Osama bin Laden" and ultimately released the visitor, sometimes erasing his camera's memory card, sometimes seizing his entire camera.

But driver Igor was a cynic. He said it was mostly the young cops.

"They dream to be General," Igor said.

And then we were there, Igor, Mirja and me standing in a cannon burst of snow 300 meters outside reactor number four, wind blistering our faces, clouds closed in, freezing cold in the dead center of the exclusion zone. It's a huge complex of buildings, concrete and steel, and we stood in a parking lot beside a monument. The sarcophagus, built in a hurry between May and November 1986, made the whole conglomeration look hunched over on itself in the snow and freezing, in a building where graphite once burned at over 2000 degrees celsius (3230 fahrenheit).

Reactor 4

●●●●●

13 THE OLD SARCOPHAGUS PROBLEM

Reactor 4's ill-fitting shell is just a bunch of concrete blocks, but getting the reactor inside them had to be as grim an engineering feat as you can contemplate. You can't help but be sympathetic that they built it in haste. They were trying to patch a gaping hole that exposed unalloyed radiation to open air.

Trouble is, building the sarcophagus as fast as they could created a porous shield. The walls are stacks of concrete blocks a meter thick and that's all they are, just stacks of blocks, not level, not straight. The roof they've laid is one-meter steel pipes supported by the remnants of the reactor building itself. Nothing is welded together, nothing is riveted to anything else. They couldn't send riveters close enough to rivet.

The whole business is structurally unsound and filled with maybe a thousand square meters of gaps and cracks. Rainwater seeps through the cracks and then the wet, radioactive air corrodes the three main structural beams from the original shelter.

About three weeks before our visit a portion of wall slabs and the roof of reactor 4 collapsed about fifty meters from the sarcophagus. Investigations blamed a truss failure precipitated by, among other factors, "corrosion due to precipitation."

As stop-gap measures they've put boron inside the sarcophagus to suppress any new chain reaction, and charcoal to filter some of the radioactivity from the air that escapes.

They guess that this ungainly mass of concrete and steel, this slap-dash thing we're staring at now, would collapse in a 6.0 Richter earthquake, a once-a-century probability in Polissia. That would lift radioactive clouds around the world all over again.

A Norwegian NGO suggested that if the collapse this past February had happened in summer when the building didn't have a cover of snow, that too would have created a contaminated dust plume.

•••••

14 THE NEW SAFE CONFINEMENT SOLUTION

A new sarcophagus, an elegant arch, is due to be completed in 2015, led by a consortium of big French construction and engineering companies called Novarka. They call it the New Safe Confinement (NSC) to differentiate it from the current structure, which just contains radioactive gases. The NSC is meant to confine the entire sarcophagus so that engineers can dismantle and decontaminate it, the reactor, the grounds, everything.

This thing is really, really big. It will stand 110 meters (360 feet) high, 250 meters (820 feet) wide, 150 meters (492 feet) long, weigh some 30,000 tons, and it's perfectly ingenious. The scheme will use giant jacks to hoist a metal exostructure high enough to cover the old structure, then slide the whole stadium-sized NSC on tracks right over the top of the old sarcophagus.

Ukraine took bids to clean up the reactor site and the winning Novarka bid was the only one of 394 entries to propose the over-the-top approach. They reckon it will protect the reactor for 100 years, long enough to take apart and clean up the mess inside.

The design challenges were formidable. Radiation levels increase higher in the air, making it unsafe to work above about thirty meters (98 feet). Yet the “internal height,” or the “bottom of the top” of the arch must reach 92.5 meters (303.5 feet) so remotely operated cranes can work inside to deconstruct the concrete, steel and debris, everything they put in place with so much haste in the first months after the accident.

How do they stay on the ground and build something a football field tall? First they build the top of the arch on the ground.

"We then attach some legs to that, which are the next part down. The structure is then jacked 30m into the air, the legs swing in and are tied together to prevent them from spreading out flat. We remove the jacks, add another pair of legs, jack that up another 30m and the process is repeated until we get the arch structure 110m up in the air," Dr. Eric Schmieman, senior technical advisor for the new sarcophagus project, told a British trade journal called *The Engineer*.

Because of deliberate, sustained remediation work over twenty years, relatively low radiation levels on the ground allow engineers to work shifts up to 40 hours a week. In fact, Schmieman says dose levels are lower than in his office back in Washington state, where the local geology is responsible for higher background radiation.

Which sounds properly swashbuckling. But less than a kilometer away, if left alone the remains of reactor 4 will need to be covered for some 20,000 more years.

•••••

On this day the first half of the arch rose out of the snow on the other side of the parking lot. In the spring they were due to add legs in sections until they had half the arch. Then they'd do it all over again and bolt the two halves together.

The NSC, left, and reactor 4, right

After that, once they get the cranes in the top of the arch, there's the little matter of getting the whole apparatus, one of the largest moving land structures in the world, the 600 meters from over there to over here. Schmieman says that should take two days.

“People ask how do you slide this thing?” said Schmieman, ‘There’s 30,000 tonnes of structural steel, it must take a lot of energy to get this going. But we’ve reduced friction enough that our concern is not about how we get it going, it’s how do we stop it, and how do we prevent it from moving before we want to because there’s a huge surface area for the wind to act on here.’

So they’ll fit the shelter with a hydraulic pawl and ratchet system to move it along the rail.

“These devices have to be perfectly coordinated,” said Schmieman. “This thing is 250m wide, we don’t want to get one side going faster than the other, just a small deviation would stop you from going any further.”

•••••

15 KURSK

The Soviet Union was epic, everything about it: The eleven time zones, the gulag archipelago, the battle of Stalingrad. And the largest tank battle in history.

The Russian town of Kursk is as patriotic and conservative as anywhere in Oklahoma. Its 415,000 people live and work in the chernozym, or black earth between Kyiv and the Russian town of Voronezh. In the summer of 1943, 7,500 Russian and Nazi tanks faced off in those fields. A glorious Soviet defensive stand made the battle of Kursk legend.

Fifty years later the Soviet Union bestowed the heroic name on one of its best-class subs. At 154 meters (505 feet), Oscar II subs were the largest cruise missile submarines in the world.

Two years before a dollar would buy 206 rubles but by the time they finished building the Kursk in October of 1994 it would buy almost 4,000. Russia was broke. Soldiers went unpaid. Military infrastructure went to ground and much of Russia's Northern Fleet rusted at anchor.

In a war game in 2000 a torpedo exploded inside the Kursk, sinking the sub. Impact with the sea bed triggered another blast 135 seconds later. One, maybe both of the explosions drove debris through the ship. The Kursk sat 108 meters down on the bottom of the Barents Sea.

The head-banging woe came from the way all hands, all 118 crew died. 23 survived the sinking. For more than two days they holed up in the undamaged tip of the ship and banged out an SOS on the hull.

Surrounded by friendly ships, they had every right to expect rescue, but as it played out Russian crews didn't have the equipment they needed to open the hatch of their own submarine.

Again the Kremlin dithered.

Should a superpower ask for help? The British offered; the Russians didn't reply.

For reasons obscure they turned to Norway, and on the ninth day, the Norwegians docked with the sub, fashioned a tool for opening the hatch and found all the sailors of the Kursk dead.

A team from the Netherlands handled salvage. Everybody was afraid that disturbing the wreck might trigger further explosions. The Russians insisted that the sub carried no nuclear warheads. Not everybody believed them.

The jacks used to lift the New Safe Confinement, the future Chernobyl sarcophagus, are the same ones the Dutch used to raise the Kursk from the bottom of the Barents sea in 2001. Dr. Eric Schmieman, the NSC technical advisor, said, “They haven’t had any use for these things since then.”

•••••

16 PRIPYAT FINDS OUT

Welcome to Pripyat

A whitewashed sign announced Pripyat in big block letters on the other side of reactor 4. 1970, it read. For most of the day we were the only people we saw, and nobody was around, so Igor stopped in the middle of the road.

Had we heard of the Red Forest?

These Scotch pines were the most contaminated patch on the planet that night in 1986. They were, essentially, fried. Radiation poured from the reactor and coursed over this spot and across the next 4,000 acres of pine trees. It was the deadliest radioactivity that escaped from reactor 4, and background radiation levels around the Red Forest remain the highest in the exclusion zone.

Igor looked over the seat: "We are now in Red Forest area. Highly contaminated but road is clean because soil was removed. It was just normal forest, pine tree forest and huge cloud of radiation arrived here. And in few weeks all trees were died because of radiation and from green color became red and brown color. Our government decide to cut and bury, so now red forest is under ground because of fire.

"All those trees became dried, you know? And in fire radiation could move out far on wind. But now you can see some trees, dried trees. It is remains from red forest. Government did not cut those trees because they died later."

They cut and buried the first dead trees because a fire there, say, set by lightning, would have awful consequences, lifting radiation into the air and carrying it away, again.

You can see the Red Forest from the "Bridge of Death." It's just a little bridge, but because it's raised above the level of the road, people came in unguarded curiosity to watch the fire burn that night in reactor 4.

The Igors doubted that many people came, that first night at least, because it happened at 1:23 in the morning. Like they said, even if someone called to tell them there was a fire, most people would probably go back to sleep.

(The Igors never tried to minimize the scope of the disaster. Evidence was everywhere, after all.)

The people of Pripyat got no word from their government for more than 24 hours, but talk spread like the radiation all day. Most who lived here were intimately connected with the workings of a nuclear plant, after all. People in a position to know.

Lyudmilla Ignatenko, newlywed wife of Vasily Ignatenko, a fireman who died fighting the reactor fire said:

"We lived in the dormitory of the fire station where he worked. On the second floor. There were three other young couples, we all shared a kitchen. On the first floor they kept the trucks. The red fire trucks. That was his job. I always knew what was happening - where he was, how he was.

"One night I heard a noise. I looked out the window. He saw me. 'Close the window and go back to sleep. There's a fire at the reactor. I'll be back soon.'

"I didn't see the explosion itself. Just the flames. Everything was radiant. The whole sky. A tall flame. And smoke. The heat was awful. And he's still not back."

That quote comes from *Voices from Chernobyl* by Ukrainian journalist Svetlana Alexievich. It is a searing book, and you are not left unsullied for reading it.

Oleg and Misha Telyatnikov (ages 12 and 10) remember their mother woke them around 3:30 Saturday morning and told them, "We are going to Kiev." Her husband was the Chernobyl fire chief.

One mother said she found the vegetable market closed on Saturday morning, and there learned of the accident. She rushed to pick up her son at school (the Soviet Union held school on Saturdays) and found the school doors locked and school officials unwilling to let the children out into the air.

Anna Kaslova, meanwhile, beamed at the very idea that she lived in Pripyat. The village she grew up in got electricity less than twenty years before.

Marianne Barisonek writes that Anna, a young mother, helped out at the Young Pioneers, a club for Soviet kids. Her husband worked at the power plant.

After he went off to work on Saturday Anna planned to take the kids to plant potatoes, but when they went outside to the bus stop, something was wrong. Ankle deep foam stood in the street. Men with cotton masks sprayed water on the buildings.

Anna and the kids waited at the bus stop but the bus didn't come, and when military vehicles started rolling through the streets she took everybody inside. Her husband called from the plant and suggested she take the kids to a resort outside of town.

Anna and her kids were already gone when they evacuated Pripyat. Because of that, they could never return home. Their time at the bus stop, in the open air, led to hospital stays for Anna and her kids. Her son Victor was diagnosed with thyroid cancer six years later. Thyroid cancer rates in Chernobyl-contaminated areas are estimated at ten times the rest of the world.

•••••

In *The Legacy of Chernobyl*, Zhores Medvedev tells the story of Lyubov Kovalevskaya, at the time of the accident a reporter for *Tribuna Enerhetyky*, the Chernobyl plant newspaper. When she woke on Saturday morning her mother told her she'd heard noises from the direction of the reactor overnight. She said the same thing Anna Kaslova said.

"All the roads were covered in water and some white liquid. Everything was white, foamy, all the curbs...I walked further and saw a policeman here, another there, I had never seen so many policemen in the town. They weren't doing anything, just sitting in various places, at the post office, the Palace of Culture. As if there was martial law. It was quite a shock. But people were walking about normally, there were children everywhere. It was very hot. People were going to the beach, to their country cottages, many people were already there, or sitting by the stream next to the cooling reservoir. That's an artificial water reservoir next to the nuclear power station...Anya, my daughter, had gone to school. I went home and said, 'Mama, I don't know what has happened, but don't let Natasha (my niece) out of the house, and when Anya returns from school, take her straight into the house'. But I didn't tell her to close the window....

“We knew nothing all day. Nobody said anything. Well, they said there was a fire. But about radiation, that radioactivity was escaping, there was not a word. Anya came back from school and said, 'Mama, we had physical exercise outside for almost a whole hour.' Insanity."

Kovalevskaya went on, “I went back to the central square.... The reactor was quite visible, one could see that it was burning and that its wall was broken. There were flames above the hole.”

Even so, even with that, life went on like a normal Saturday. Because it was unseasonably warm gardeners readied their plots for springtime. Children played in the sun. People were wed in Chernobyl Saturday night.

•••••

Despite official silence word got around. In *Chernobyl and its aftermath,* Robert E. Ebel writes that “notices were posted in some apartment buildings” on Sunday morning, and “there is evidence that indicates that guidance went out over local radio Saturday afternoon, well before the decision to evacuate had been made, telling everyone to stay indoors.”

Nadezhda Makarenko watched Vremya on TV Saturday night. It didn't mention the accident, but at 9:30 somebody pounded on the door.

"We are from the city civilian defense," they told her. "Take a tablet for each member of your family. Take it without fail. It is a protection against radiation. Nothing dangerous has happened but in any event, it is necessary as a prophylactic, don't open the air vent, and everything will be better."

Just after 6:00 Sunday morning a woman moved from apartment to apartment telling residents, "Turn your radio up full blast! Don't leave your home, and don't open the window!"

At 13:10, the local radio news reader, Nina Melnick, interrupted a program from Moscow. She wanted to sound calm but her voice shook.

"There has been an accident at our nuclear power station. We ask you to be calm. Gather up your necessary things, what you need for three days, food and clothing. At 1400 hours a bus will be sent to your home, and you are to take a seat on it."

The official announcement read like this:

"For the attention of the residents of Pripyat! The City Council informs you that due to the accident at Chernobyl Power Station in the city of Pripyat the radioactive conditions in the vicinity are deteriorating. The Communist Party, its officials and the armed forces are taking necessary steps to combat this. Nevertheless, with the view to keep people as safe and healthy as possible, the children being top priority, we need to temporarily evacuate the citizens in the nearest towns of Kiev Oblast. For these reasons, starting from April 27, 1986 2 pm each apartment block will be able to have a bus at its disposal, supervised by the police and the city officials. It is highly advisable to take your documents, some vital personal belongings and a certain amount of food, just in case, with you. The senior executives of public and industrial facilities of the city has decided on the list of employees needed to stay in Pripyat to maintain these facilities in a good working order. All the houses will be guarded by the police during the evacuation period. Comrades, leaving your residences temporarily please make sure you have turned off the lights, electrical equipment and water and shut the windows. Please keep calm and orderly in the process of this short-term evacuation."

•••••

Valeri Sluckij, his wife Natalia and their two children must have heard Nina Melnick on the radio. When they found out, they had forty minutes to evacuate their fourth floor apartment on Stroytely Street. Thinking they would soon be back, they brought five plastic bags with their various papers, Natalia's English textbooks, some novels and cutlery.

"We thought we were coming back, so we just took a few things," Sluckij told Adam Higginbotham in the London Observer. Sluckij stole back to Pripyat over the years. Across the empty town the street lights would still come on. That, he said, was frightening.

•••••

17 EVACUATE!

You can blame Moscow for just about everything, from the fatal experiment itself to its subsequent opacity before the rest of the world, right through to the very design of the reactor. But they put on a pretty good evacuation, in two hours and twenty minutes start to finish.

Compared to the national leadership, local officials seized up with panic in an epic fail. They didn't keep people indoors. Some tried to hide the accident entirely. Some officials scoffed at worried residents, "(A)ren't you used to that? It was a steam discharge from the power plant," according to PBS's Nova.

At the plant, bosses froze in place, eyes wide, far out of their depth. For the first day they misrepresented the severity of the emergency to Moscow and throughout they underestimated the calamity at hand. It took national officials arriving from the capital to comprehend the catastrophe.

Moscow got to Pripyat fast. An investigating committee of ministers and deputies, among them the electric power minister, the first deputy health minister and the first deputy director of Russia's main nuclear research body left the capital for Kyiv at 16:00 Saturday afternoon. The senior politician on the committee, deputy premier Boris Y. Shcherbina, was traveling elsewhere and flew to Pripyat separately.

The Moscow contingent made the decision to evacuate Pripyat late Saturday night, a few hours after their arrival and just 20 or 21 hours after the blast. The civil defense and medical people insisted on it.

Deputy Health Minister Yevgeny I. Vorobyev railed, beside himself. "Evacuation is necessary at once! There is plutonium, cesium, strontium ... in the air. The condition of the casualties in the medical unit indicates very intense radiation fields. The thyroid glands of people, including children, have been larded with radioactive iodine.

No one is doing prevention with potassium iodide .... Incredible ...!"

And still the fire in reactor 4 burned intensely, incredibly hot. It's strange, but that probably spared Pripyat, for the heat rose as if through a smokestack, lifting radioactive dust and particles a kilometer into the air, far above and beyond town.

Since the initial radiation sailed high over Pripyat and away some of the Moscow committee hoped radiation levels would settle down before they'd have to evacuate. But the initial blast calmed down and the wind changed direction during the night prompting the decision, nominally made by the head of Moscow's scientific team, a man named Valeriy Legasov. Who now had some daunting logistics to get right, and fast.

Comrade Legasov summoned transportation. Two diesel trains called at the Yanov station just west of the Bridge of Death, right up by the plant, providing 1500 seats. The team calculated the number of people in an apartment building times the 23 buildings, divided by the number of seats on a bus and guessed they'd need something like twelve hundred buses. Calls went out. Before dawn a queue of big yellow city buses began to assemble outside town, driven up from Kyiv.

Officials asked for volunteer drivers and some of the confirmed cases of radiation sickness were among bus drivers who thought the whole business was a lark. They drove up from Kyiv Saturday night and hung out, played soccer with the other drivers and stood and watched the reactor burn, knowing nothing of the danger.

Unfortunately for the evacuation effort, reactor 4 is right between Pripyat and Kiev and the only road connecting the two, the same road Igor brought us in on, runs right over the Bridge of Death and right past the reactor.

Under the circumstances, it was going to have to do. It was better than herding the whole town onto the radioactive train platform.

In fact, the evacuation team caught a series of huge breaks. If the U.S.S.R.'s third largest city hadn't been a scant 110 kilometers (70 miles) down the road with the resources that come with a population of 2.3 million people the evacuation would have taken far longer.

The Soviets' lag in consumer culture also played to the planners' benefit. Because few people had cars or houses the evacuation moved forward in buses from apartment blocks, an efficient combination for which the authorities could thank their lucky red stars.

Beginning thirty six hours after the accident they evacuated Pripyat, quickly and calmly under the eyes of the militia. Once the evacuation finally started they got everybody out in under three hours. Authorities said 1,216 buses and 300 trucks were used. The convoy stretched twenty kilometers along the entire road from Pripyat back to Chernobyl.

No one thought to change the bus tires at the edge of the zone. Radioactivity measured on the asphalt required them to wash down the roads in Kyiv for months.

•••••

In the Soviet Union the waiting list for little East German Trabant sedans was ten years in 1987. It was up to fifteen years for domestic Ladas and Czechoslovakian Skodas. Not many people in Pripyat had their own car in 1986. Those who did were naturally keen to flee in their cars and not the buses. With your car, you could take more of your things. You could take your pets.

Maybe that's why the authorities told people they'd only be away for a few days. In the panic that would follow the truth, people would try to bring out more things, and slow down the evacuation. And besides, they'd be carrying every kind of radioactive thing out into the larger population.

Though some made it out of town with their cars, the government forbade it. Everyone had to take the buses. Family dogs ran after the buses for a distance, then fell back. They sent in hunters with shotguns and a tableau of heartbreak spread across Pripyat as corpses of radioactive pets lined the streets. A month later a hundred mile perimeter of barbed wire and watchtowers spanned the exclusion zone, gulag-style. Not to keep people in, but to make sure they stayed out.

•••••

Beyond getting people outside the ten kilometer circle (the 30 k zone came later) nobody had done a lot of planning. An evacuee named G. N. Petrov told Grigoriy Medvedev:

"We drove to Ivankov (60 km from Pripyat) and there were scattered among the villages. Not everyone took us in willingly. One well-off peasant would not let my family into his immense brick house, not because of the dangerous radiation (he did not understand about that, and explanations had no effect on him), but out of greed. He had not built it, he said, to let strangers in....

"Many who had left the buses in Ivankov went on further toward Kiev by foot. Some hitched rides. A helicopter pilot I knew told me only later what he had seen from the air: huge crowds of lightly dressed people, women with children, elderly people, going along the road and the shoulders toward Kiev."

•••••

Valeriy Legasov, lead scientist on Moscow's Chernobyl team and the man who ordered the evacuation, presented the Soviet report to the International Atomic Energy Agency in August. He may have been more forthright than his government preferred. His western colleagues appreciated his candor but back home he was passed over twice for recognition as a Hero of Socialist Labor. The second time, it was said, under instruction from on high.

In failing health possibly due to radiation (after they made the decision to evacuate Pripyat Legasov, Shcherbina the deputy premier and Gennady Shasharin, a Soviet energy official, took a helicopter ride over the open, burning reactor), on the second anniversary of the accident Legasov hanged himself from the stairwell of his apartment.

The Kurchatov Institute, where Legasov was First Deputy Director, designed the flawed Chernobyl-type reactor. After his suicide they acknowledged the control rod design problem, and fixed it.

•••••

18 THE WORLD FINDS OUT

It was anything but just another Monday at the Forsmark power station, 116 kilometers (72 miles) north of Stockholm. At 9:00 a.m. an alarm went out from reactor 1. Arriving employees' shoes tested radioactive. They checked the ground outside and it registered radioactive, too.

So they began to evacuate. Lars Wahlström, the radiation supervisor, said, "Rumors about the activity circulated between noon and 14 hours and people said 'Now let's leave here.' At the same time news arrived that radioactivity had been detected in Finland."

In time they realized the whole east coast was contaminated. Wahlström wasn't sure anything at all was wrong at Forsmark.

"We had even been inside the chimney and checked.... and by around 15.30 it was determined that the fallout definitely did not come from Forsmark." At first they suspected a nuclear plant at Ignalino in Lithuania, which is much closer to Sweden than Chernobyl.

•••••

Moscow hadn't said a word. They knew, though. They scrambled aircraft to monitor the radioactive cloud from the beginning. First the cloud crossed into Poland and then Finland. Finland recorded increased background radiation at a measuring station at Kajaani, right in the center of the country, but it turned out Finland wasn't as stricken as other Nordic countries. The bulk of the cloud floated over Finland's lakes and forests unimpeded by rain, more than a kilometer in the air. Migrating birds, though, on the way back from wintering in east Africa, arrived around Finnish lakes coated with fallout.

Neither was fallout so bad in Norway. They found contaminated lettuce in spring, and by slaughter season, reindeer meat and mutton tested contaminated. They were prohibited for sale.

Sweden had the bum luck. Rain fell north of Stockholm on Monday and Tuesday, bringing radiation down with it. Gävle was a regional center of 70,000, some 200 kilometers (124 miles) up the E-4 from Stockholm (not far from the Forsmark power station), a harbor town bordering the Bay of Bothnia in the Baltic Sea (and home to Gevalia coffee). For two harvest years vegetables couldn't be sold and pastures couldn't be grazed in the countryside around Gävle. It cost Sweden a hundred million dollars.

Chernobyl entirely changed the lives of the Sami, an indigenous herding, fishing and trapping people who live mostly across the northern regions of Norway, Sweden, Finland and European Russia. Some 70,000 semi-nomadic Sami follow reindeer in their regular migration. They depend on them for food, clothing and livelihood.

The serious trouble didn't begin right away but rather a few months later, in autumn. When snows cover the grasses, the Sami change their reindeer to a winter diet of lichen, dug from under the snow.

Reactor 4 ejected the isotope cesium 137 which contaminated the fish the Sami fished, the game they trapped and the reindeer they herded, but most harmfully it contaminated lichen, which don't have roots, and so extract their food directly from the air. Lichen soaked in airborne cesium 137 and passed it straight on to the deer.

Faced with the impossible choice of destroying the Sami way of life or protecting its larger population, the Swedish government ordered nearly 80% of all reindeer meat in the country destroyed in 1986, and 29% in 1987. Sweden imported clean reindeer meat for the Sami to eat, ironically mostly from the largely unaffected Russian Kola peninsula, the area around Murmansk.

Pieces of debris from the reactor core traveled through the air all the way to Poland, the most affected country besides the Soviet Union. The Moscow-allied government in Warsaw didn't release official maps or statistics, but they were the only European government to distribute iodine tablets to children.

In early May fresh milk tested contaminated and was banned for sale in Hungary. Spinach and salad greens were destroyed in Austria, and milk distribution to schools and the sale of some vegetables there were halted. Heavy showers in southern Germany from April 29th to May 2nd brought contamination to Munich, where most green vegetables had to be destroyed.

Rain in early May brought radiation down on Ireland, north Wales and Scotland, where the sale of some three million sheep and lambs for meat was prohibited, though wool production continued. I was in Moscow in July, and the U.S.

government advised everyone in our group to avoid eating leafy vegetables.

•••••

19 A WALK IN THE SNOW

Driver Igor didn't so much park as execute a slow hip check on a snow pile where he then spent most of the day sitting in the Lacetti by himself. Nobody else in the parking lot. Nobody else on the town square. Nobody here but us. Igor the guide, Mirja and I set out to spend the day hiking up Lenin Street and back exploring the abandoned city.

Hotel Polissia, Pripyat

Cast your eyes over the Pripyat town square. City hall, a supermarket, restaurants, the Palace of

Culture, the Polissya Hotel. Nobody living here for 27 years but somebody ran a big bold brand new Soviet hammer and sickle flag up the pole over by the Polissya Hotel. Nice touch.

We made our own footpaths in the snow, right down the middle of boulevards built in the Soviet style - big and broad to make you feel small. You could double that because of the ghostliness of the place and the lack of other people, and Lenin Street felt all the wider because there were no vehicles.

Eventually they buried Pripyat's cars and trucks in several places, one of them called Rossokha. Igor the driver put it this way: "Private car stay here. After accident we measure car. If this car not contaminated, clean, okay, you can go outside. But if too much radiation, buried here."

You can't visit Rossokha anymore. It's only 20 kilometers southwest of Chernobyl and it used to be they'd take you there but five years ago they stopped it. Some 12,000 helicopters, compactors, trucks, cement trucks, excavators, tanks and APCs, bulldozers and cranes from every corner of the Soviet Union came to Chernobyl in the course of the cleanup. They usually ended up at Rossokha, where radiation levels remained high 22 years later, as high as 300 microSieverts an hour, a potentially lethal dose in about a day. Still people came and looted for parts until the zone administration finally had a fit and stopped visits to Rossokha altogether. Ultimately they buried everything.

•••••

Odd. The signs above the fruit and vegetable sections at the supermarket held their bright blue color after all this time. The front of the store wasn't even there but the signs looked good as new. The ceiling cladding had fallen away revealing sagging ductwork, but some fluorescent light fixtures still hung attached to metal. A few bulbs literally hung in there. The snow played over upturned shopping carts, forlorn and half covered by drifts.

Supermarket, Pripyat

We walked right through the Palace of Culture and out the back. The white stuff blew into the building and icicles hung over the basketball court. The backboard was up there, but no hoop. Igor said he wouldn't ordinarily take us through that way, but since there was nobody else here, and it was cold as could be, and it was a quicker way to the amusement park....

The palace of culture, Pripyat

If you were eight years old the amusement park must have looked great in 1986, but a kid would flee screaming this morning. Wide, open, windswept and rusted, bumper cars, a gondola ride, a swinging paratrooper-type thing and the iconic ferris wheel stood frozen in time and temperature. The gondolas should have swung in the wind but they were rusted still.

The ferris wheel

The Pripyat amusement park

The playground had the highest radiation of the day. Igor knelt to hold the dosimiter near the ground and this is where it showed 8.65 microSieverts per hour.

He brought us here to show us, because he knew it was always high right here. But why this little patch of ground between the bumper cars and the paratroopers?

Igor the scientist turned up his broad hands.

“Who knows?” His eyes searched ours.

Rescue and cleanup helicopters set down on this expanse of concrete in the aftermath. It was ready made for that. Cleanup workers, the liquidators, must have washed radiation off of the concrete and into the soil, so the tarmac parts of the plaza are relatively clean compared to the edges of the park.

•••••

You had to walk gingerly up the steps to swimming pool Lazurny (Azure) because broken glass littered the floor and as Mirja said, a broken ankle from slipping on the ice and the glass in here would be a big problem.

The front door laid in the snow under some branches, busted clean out of the entranceway. Icicles hung a meter below the edge of the landing. Bushy brown grass (tall as amber waves of grain) bunched up alongside the icicles up on the roof, like on country houses in Norway.

Entrance to swimming pool Lazurny, left

Baby blue paint peeled from the two-tier Olympic-style diving board into a massively deep deep end. Five forlorn starting blocks lined up underneath.

Torn and ragged canvas dangled from the ceiling, which otherwise showed a matrix of rusty bars. Icicles hung from the open windows, and from branches that leaned inside. Graffiti insulted the tiles around the bottom of the pool.

Swimming pool Lazurny

Swimming pool Lazurny stayed open for years after the accident for the liquidators, the scientists and the others who remained behind. They finally shut the doors in 1998, or 1997 or when the rest of the reactors were finally shut down (December, 2000), depending on your source.

Igor swam here well after the accident, starting as soon as he got his scientist job. He took this place personally. Standing in here, in the aquatics center all busted and bereft, he lamented the bad people who wrecked it. Sadness flashed across his face and you could feel his sorrow.

•••••

In Pripyat Middle School #3, the walls of the corridor, plastered over in their day, had returned to brick and mortar, the plaster falling away only a little more slowly than the peeling paint. Neither rhyme nor reason prevailed, but rather randomness and chaos. Light fixtures once held fluorescent bulbs, but they'd long since been stripped. Except wait, now and again a bulb leaned up against the wall. A 55 gallon drum rested heavy on its side, rusted, and a metal ladder, same condition, leaned against it.

Pripyat Middle School #3

Those old enough to remember the Soviet Union will remember photos of comrades lined up to read the latest issues of Pravda or Izvestia, displayed behind glass in public places. A yellowed copy of the semi-weekly newspaper Soviet Patriot hung on the wall still protected behind glass. A broadsheet, it was pulled open to its front and back pages, which fit just so into a wooden frame.

A project for wood shop, maybe. This issue was dated Wednesday, 23 April, 1986. The accident happened in the first hours of Saturday the 26th.

Soviet Patriot, 23 April, 1986

In the next classroom, a long one, all of the windows stood open and I couldn't quite work out why. They were tall windows, the kind that swung open to one side, and as we picked our way along,

I counted an even dozen frames, each gathering little snow drifts, one after the other.

Another corridor, more windows. Hard-backed metal chairs against the walls with science posters above them. Schoolbooks all over the floor outside of room 202. One was open to a map that would fire a schoolboy's imagination. It showed the BAM, or Baikal Amur Mainline, a true Soviet engineering accomplishment, a rail line north of the Trans-Siberian to impossibly exotic destinations like Bratsk and Tynda that was finished just two years before the accident.

Posters showed the surface of the moon, with drawings of how a future Soviet expeditionary robot might get around. There were posters about engines. Posters about space flight. Pencil drawings of, I imagine, venerated Soviet scientists. Big lecture rooms. A soft chair and more hard-backed ones. Illustrations of Lenin gazing forward. Illustrations of Lenin exhorting. The peeling paint in this classroom was green.

Pripyat Middle School #3

Next door the same windows as before were all shut, but no matter. There was no glass in any window in either room. In the cafeteria, dozens and dozens of gas masks covered the floor, most of them busted apart, the hose torn from the mask. My best guess is that they were kept elsewhere in the school and later strewn about by vandals or perhaps by photographers to add melodrama to their work. A few masks hung from hooks on the walls.

The cafeteria and kitchen in Middle School #3

Whether photo props or not, they stood in unvarnished testimony to the dead seriousness of Soviet civil defense drills circa 1986. And given where we were, the complete quiet, and the condition of everything around us, they were downright creepy.

At one side of the cafeteria the kitchen, modular serving stations and vents for stoves slumped in rusty paralysis. An old cooking pot leaned against the wall.

On the other side all those masks covered the floor, and tables stood haphazardly against one another. Two rusty green cash registers with mechanical buttons sat among the masks.

The one that still had a display showed 31.20 rubles, a lot of money, about fifty dollars in 1986. In a school cafeteria, what could that have been for?

31.20 Rubles

Igor told us we could visit a typical abandoned flat, but in the end time ran out. After tramping up and down Pripyat town we had to go, because everybody's got to eat, or at least every tour feels like it ought to offer a meal, and soon they were due to close the canteen back at ChernobylInterInform.

I expect our Igors were determined not to miss it (they both ate eagerly). So we all headed back to the edge of the exclusion zone for an indifferent meal, indifferently served.

Chernobyl InterInform's cafeteria

Everybody else's heads were already in their soup bowls when we arrived - the Norwegians with Misha, the eighteen from the bus. Borscht with some Ukrainian version of quinoa was pretty good. The rest was not. They made a point to say that the ingredients came from outside the zone.

•••••

20 GETTING OUT

At both the Leliv (ten kilometer) and Dytyatky (thirty kilometer) checkpoints everybody, guides included, headed into buildings to be radiation-checked. Hands and feet. You stood on a platform and straddled a machine sideways and held your hands flat to a panel on each side to check what you'd been in contact with. The thing took a reading and the gate on the other side would open if you passed.

A higher level of radiation would open the door at Leliv than at Dytyatky, which was at the outer gate to the exclusion zone. If a tourist's radiation level were too high it would be trouble for his guide, not so much for the tourist. They'd want to know whether the guide allowed the tourist out of his sight, whether they might have been in a woods or somewhere else they shouldn't have, and they would disassemble the offender's clothing one item at a time starting with the shoes to find the over-irradiated item.

There is a story everyone has heard but no one seems to be able to verify about one man being naked before the guards learned he once underwent radiation therapy for cancer.

•••••

The drive up to Chernobyl took just shy of two hours. The drive back took a lot less, with less snow and a lot more overtaking. Judging from our Igors, real Ukrainians don't wear seat belts.

Out in the middle somewhere Igor got a traffic ticket. It came from a radar trap, a freezing cop in a little Lada like the one we passed on the way up. We were approaching a village, see, where the speed limit drops, and 74 kph in a 50 kph zone will cost you 260 Hryvna, something more than thirty dollars.

We wanted to know. Would the cop take a cash bribe?

“Of course, this is Ukraine,” Igor the driver said.

Maybe he would take 200. But if Igor offered it, it wouldn’t be to save 60 hryvna. What it would save him was time. He’d pay it to avoid the consarned bureaucracy.

Otherwise he’d have to go to the bank to pay the fee, then go to the police station to show them he’d paid, so a bribe might save him a whole day’s pay at work. The system, he said, is made for bribing.

Maybe the cop would take the bribe and maybe he wouldn’t, Igor thought, because after all he didn’t know who he was stopping and it could be another cop who might report him. Either way though, the cop was making $400 a month and he had a family to feed, so Igor had no complaint. The cop did what he had to do. That the bribee has fundamental sympathy for the briber, seems to me that doesn’t augur well.

•••••

21 REVELATIONS

Naturally, crazy, juicy theories rose from the Chernobyl apocalypse. First, it was all foretold in the Book of Revelations: "And the third angel sounded, and there fell a great star from heaven, burning as it were a lamp, and it fell upon the third part of the rivers, and upon the fountains of waters; And the name of the star is called Wormwood: and the third part of the waters became wormwood; and many men died of the waters, because they were made bitter." - Revelation 8:10-11

"Chornobyl" is the Ukrainian word for wormwood. In her book *Wormwood Forest* Mary Mycio says chornobyl is a plant called Artemisia vulgaris, a near cousin to "wormwood," or Artemisia absinthium, which is a hardy perennial with leaves with fine silky hairs that give it a whitish tinge. Mycio says they are "everywhere" in the exclusion zone.

We have to take her word for it. If they are they were buried under the snow.

Besides Revelations, there is some nice Christian legend intertwined with wormwood. It's bitter and a natural repellant of flies, worms and fleas. In the lore, when the biblical serpent was expelled from Eden, wormwood sprang up on the trail to prevent its return.

Then there's Zbigniew Jaworowski, physician, mountain climber, and chairman of the Scientific Council of the Central Laboratory for Radiological Protection in Warsaw. He held (he died in 2011) that there was never any need to evacuate and there have been no cancers attributable to Chernobyl. Made a name for himself.

All those stories about thyroid cancer in the villages in the exclusion zone? A hoax.

You'll find his supporters on the internet.

And finally, the grand geopolitical conspiracy. Igor the driver relished telling it.

The United States was behind the explosion, naturally. The Challenger space shuttle exploded 88 days before the accident at reactor 4. Conspiracy types on the Soviet home team claimed victory for Challenger's demise. Then came Chernobyl, so it was obviously American revenge, especially since the Americans sat in fear of awesome Soviet progress in the sciences.

•••••

Ukraine is a poor country with a laundry list of problems including government corruption and an insular reluctance to connect with the rest of the world. So what to do with the brooding, leaden legacy of Chernobyl?

Over time, notions that visiting Chernobyl is "disaster tourism" may change. As the danger ebbs, specialist tours will emerge. Some will visit to see the wildlife and nature, others to see the reactor and so on. As half-lives shorten it will become less unusual to visit Chernobyl.

But Ukraine and Belarus have scarce money to jump start the process, so it won't be easy, or fast. Modern day squatters may creep back into the radioactivity where a ruble or a hryvna is to be made, and chances are the government back in Minsk or Kyiv won't come and uproot them.

I've read about a dozen people's trips to Chernobyl. Everybody warns of the dangers, cites the statistics, wags all the fingers. But they also go right ahead and do it. So did we.

We stood there in the snow at reactor 4 and Igor showed us the level of microSieverts on his dosimeter, and for a day it was all just science words, and since I didn't feel anything the rules didn't apply to me.

And some of the people in the aftermath thought they didn't apply to them either. The 200-odd remaining samosely, or "self-settlers," the old people who moved back home, continue to discount all the facts about radiation and live here today, right now. Enough people that the

Emergency Ministry runs a van every week selling provisions.

But they are old and infirm, and no younger people are moving in to replace them.

Compare and contrast with the Chernobyl engineers who packed Pripyat, the fruit of Soviet education, carrying slide rules and boring their wives with their science and supplying ten per cent of Ukraine's power from this little place, chock full of facts, figures, problems and solutions.

Those young men and women were focused. Narrow, clinical. It was all there in facts and figures, ma'am, and they pored over them for a living, all day and all night, and they sifted through them all and then on the fateful day they blew each other up.

•••••

Everything is more plausible when you're there. People in Nepal venerate the Kumari, a living child goddess who loses her goddess status at adolescence.

You hire a guy to show you around Kathmandu. He's older than you and his slacks are nicer than your jeans and he presents as a reasonable enough fellow, and he takes you to the Kumari's house and tells you the story. You gaze up at the Kumari's balcony and you're skeptical, but this guy's an evangelist, so you give the Kumari a few more minutes of the time of day.

What's curious is, the dark and brooding Chernobyl isn't more plausible now that I've gone to see it. It's cheerless, sure, but try as I might I can't conjure Chernobyl into a malicious act by evil men. It was an accident and a disaster too. But it came from striving in the name of science for good. To harness nature and improve the lot of the country.

Those who have come back since the accident and ripped apart and defiled the towns and villages by hand with a hard chauvinist Slavic vengeance, if you're after evil, there's your evil.

Chernobyl is a real and verdant and prolific place. It's dead to humans but plants and animals thrive. You come around to admire the old self-settlers' panache. Even if they only came back because of pure, mule-headed ignorance, they're living their lives by their own rules.

●●●●●

EPILOGUE

In the early morning of March 24, 1992, a pressure seal failed in the number 3 unit of the Leningradskaya Nuclear Power Plant at Sosnoviy Bor, releasing radioactive gases. My friend Steve and I had train tickets from Tallinn, in newly independent Estonia, to St. Petersburg a day later that would take us within twenty kilometers of the plant.

By five in the afternoon monitoring stations in Finland detected higher than normal readings. The level of iodine-131 at Lovisa, Finland, just across the gulf, was 1,000 times higher than before the accident, the German Institute for Applied Ecology said.

The local authorities reported the accident in the media, and I think they felt a little self-satisfied for doing it, but it didn't help because Russian credibility had burned down with Chernobyl's reactor 4. Any more, people thought the Soviets, as Seymour Hersh said about Henry Kissinger, lied like other people breathe. And as usual, solid information was hard to come by.

(Strictly speaking, the Soviet Union had dissolved three months before, at the start of the year, but the Russians at Sosnoviy Bor that day were firm products of the Soviet system.)

A news agency in St. Petersburg reported increased radiation, and the Swedish news reported panic in St. Petersburg. A lady in Tallinn told me her mother had called from St. Petersburg and they were closing the schools and sending children home to stay indoors.

No one believed the plant spokesman on TV when he said hey, no problem. The Finnish Prime Minister fussed that it took seven hours before the Russians told him. No one trusted the Russian version of events. It was frightening.

I was in a hotel called the Viru in Tallinn. Finnish-built, it was just about the only place foreigners stayed and something of a legend. The Viru opened in 1972 and the more adventurous Finns (whose language is similar enough to Estonian that they can understand one another) trickled in to have a look at Soviet Estonians' way of life. And so naturally, for the Viru's first twenty years the KGB spied on guests from the top floor. Today a museum up on the 23rd floor displays the listening equipment.

Tallinn was maybe the only place you could watch western TV in the USSR, broadcast from Helsinki, 50 miles (about 80 kilometers) across the Gulf of Finland.

Taru Mäkelä, who made a film about the Viru, said "Moscow boycotted the Los Angeles Olympics in 1984. The games were not televised in the Soviet Union. Then the whole of the Moscow elite travelled to the Viru hotel to watch the Olympics on Finnish television."

Finnish TV stayed on the radiation leak all day and we were glad they did. A consensus emerged on the other side of the gulf that it wasn't a big deal. The Finns had boats out measuring the air, and at Kotka up on the Finnish/Russian border they didn't measure anything at all.

The Commission on Security and Cooperation in Europe had a politicians' meeting in Helsinki that day. They showed it on Finnish TV and we decided that when that room emptied we probably ought to leave, too. And then the morning of the train the VOA radio news had the leak as about its fifth story and we believed the Americans when they told us it was okay. We took the train.

•••••

Mikhail Gorbachev used the 20th anniversary of the accident in April 2006 to finger Chernobyl as a turning point in the collapse of the Soviet Union. "The Chernobyl disaster," he wrote, "opened the possibility of much greater freedom of expression, to the point that the system as we knew it could no longer continue." He wrote that he "started to think about time in terms of pre-Chernobyl and post-Chernobyl." He protested his administration's innocence, insisting "nobody knew the truth."

"Of course, the world first learned of the Chernobyl disaster from Swedish scientists, creating the impression that we were hiding something. But in truth we had nothing to hide, as we simply had no information for a day and a half," Gorbachev wrote.

But within sixteen-odd hours of the blast Moscow's radiation hospital had 129 patients already under treatment, airlifted from the blast site. The Kremlin's hand-picked team gave the order to evacuate Pripyat less than 24 hours after the blast.

It may serve the former General Secretary to see the collapse of the USSR on his watch as caused by cataclysm, an event with effects far beyond the control of a mortal leader. But Gorbachev didn't grant the "much greater freedom of expression." Chernobyl set it in train. It rode in on the shock tide of the government's opacity with vital health information. Soviets turned appalled, then generally disgusted.

Radiation was mysterious, menacing, personal and permanent. Until now most people were good Soviet citizens like you're a good American. Only dissidents were dissidents, there weren't many of them, and nobody thought they were very important.

Chernobyl made things personal. Now it was radiation in your little girl's milk. They said the government mixed irradiated cow meat with uncontaminated beef and sold it across the land to dilute all the contaminated meat and everybody believed it. Now your government was trying to poison you.

Behind the monolith lurked only mortals, panicked and mendacious. The mask had slipped. Chernobyl punched holes through the Soviet ramparts and facts poured out.

Like Nixon with Watergate, Gorbachev preferred to change the subject. He took his show on the road, to Havana in April 1988, where Fidel Castro stroked his beard and declared, "Perestroika is another man's wife. I don't want to get involved."

The General Secretary tried releasing political prisoners. Closing one of the harshest gulag camps, Perm-35, got Mart Niklus, a zoologist and 'dangerous recidivist,' a bus ticket home to Estonia in time for mass patriotic "song festivals" that summer, and before the year was out the Estonian parliament effectively declared home rule.

The empire reeled, and at every extremity. In early 1989 Lt. General Boris Gromov's fortieth army, untold columns of troops, tanks and armored personnel carriers, slunk back across the Friendship Bridge into the Soviet Socialist Republic of Uzbekistan, bringing to a close a nine year occupation of Afghanistan that cost 15,000 Soviet lives.

Moscow's Eastern European satellites wobbled out of orbit and that autumn, fell from the Soviet sky. Gorbachev the furiously traveling salesman visited Helsinki in October. His spokesman Gannadi Gerasimov made weak light of the situation.

"You know the Frank Sinatra song, 'I Did It My Way'?" he asked reporters. "Hungary and Poland are doing it their way."

Two weeks later the Berlin Wall was down and the Soviet republics themselves had gone furiously afray. Soviet APCs dispersed a demonstration killing 20 in Tbilisi, capital of Georgia. Azerbaijani villagers beat Armenians and Armenians ejected Azeris, igniting the Nagorno-Karabakh War that lasted six years and killed 30,000. Lithuania declared independence and Soviet APCs seized the TV tower in Vilnius, killing 13. And by then it was too late. Political prisoners were out of the gulag, the cat was out of the bag and the whole shabby thing fell down.

SOURCES AND FURTHER READING

Any errors or omissions in this text are entirely my own. I am grateful to all who created the following source material, listed in alphabetical order by title. Web addresses change, but these were correct at the time of publishing. Use this list for further reading:

A Country of Women by Holly Morris in More Magazine: http://www.more.com/chernobyl-women-nuclear-holly-morris

A trip to Chernobyl from timemachine.net: http://sv-timemachine.net/2009/04/chernobyl-part-i/

Accident at Russian Sosnovy Bor-3: http://www.wiseinternational.org/node/576

Accidental Tourist, a 2003 visit to Chernobyl: http://www.smh.com.au/articles/2003/10/31/1067566074374.html

ANALYSIS: Roof collapse at Chernobyl: http://www.bellona.org/articles/articles_2013/chernobyl_roof_collapse_report

And animals walking there free...Or does Chernobyl need wildlife sanctuary? from forUm, Ukraine: http://en.for-ua.com/comments/2013/04/22/140929.html

Artemisia vulgaris on Wikipedia: http://en.wikipedia.org/wiki/Artemisia_vulgaris

At Chernobyl, Danger Lurks in the Trees: http://wwwp.dailyclimate.org/tdc-newsroom/2013/06/chernobyl-forest-fire

Back to Chernobyl on PBS's NOVA: http://www.youtube.com/watch?v=ct1NaSAmiuQ

Belarus Cursed by Chernobyl from BBC News: http://news.bbc.co.uk/2/hi/europe/4485003.stm

Black Tuesdays scar Russian economy for decades from Pravda: http://english.pravda.ru/business/finance/11-10-2012/122425-black_tuesday-0/

Building Chernobyl's New Safe Confinement by Jon Excell: http://www.theengineer.co.uk/in-depth/the-big-story/building-chernobyls-new-safe-confinement/1015479.article

Catastrophe in Chernobyl: how people live in the exclusion zone: http://news.vdok.org/page.aspx?id=4321

Cause and Effect: Understanding Chernobyl by Marianne Barisonek: http://www.amazon.com/gp/product/B004TGT3IG/

Cheating Chernobyl, an interview with Alexander Yuvchenko: http://www.ecolo.org/documents/documents_in_english/cherno-alexander_yuvchenko.htm

Chernobyl A Nuclear Disaster from ThinkQuest: http://library.thinkquest.org/3426/

Chernobyl: A Short History of the Human Impact By Lisa Horner: http://www.sras.org/chernobyl_short_history_human_impact

Chernobyl Accident and Its Consequences: http://www.nei.org/Master-Document-Folder/Backgrounders/Fact-Sheets/Chernobyl-Accident-and-Its-Consequences

Chernobyl and Pripyat by Simon Butcher: https://simon.butcher.name/archives/2008/10/25/Chernobyl-and-Pripyat

Chernobyl and The Nuclear Power Controversy from the Morningside Center for Teaching Social Responsibility: http://www.morningsidecenter.org/teachable-moment/lessons/chernobyl-nuclear-power-controversy

Chernobyl, beyond the numbers by Plutonium Page: http://thenexthurrah.typepad.com/the_next_hurrah/2006/04/it_was_like_air.html

Chernobyl: Chronology of a Disaster from Nuclear Monitor: http://www.nirs.org/mononline/nm724.pdf

Chernobyl Disaster from Wikipedia: http://en.wikipedia.org/wiki/Chernobyl_disaster

The Chernobyl Exclusion Zone from Firesuite Photography: http://www.firesuite.com/chernobyl-exclusion-zone-2008-09.html

Chernobyl Fungus Feeds on Radiation by Kate Melville in Science A Go Go: http://www.scienceagogo.com/news/20070422222547data_trunc_sys.shtml

Chernobyl: Meltdown, Explosion, Radiation and Cleaning It Up from Facts and Details: http://factsanddetails.com/world.php?itemid=2404

Chernobyl Notebook by Grigoriy Medvedev: http://www.amazon.com/gp/product/B00515LT2M/

The Chernobyl Project - The death of Vladimir Pravik: http://chernobylproject.blogspot.com/2011/08/death-of-vladimir-pravik.html

Chernobyl thirty kilometer zone map from Chernobyl Tour: http://www.chernobyl-tour.com/alles/chernobyl_30km_zone_map-www.chernobyl-tour.com.jpg

Chernobyl: Transforming an Icon by Dick Kovan: http://www2.ans.org/pubs/magazines/nn/docs/2006-4-3.pdf

Chernobyl 20 years on by Adam Higginbotham from the Guardian: http://www.theguardian.com/world/2006/mar/26/nuclear.russia

Chernobyl 25 years on: a poisoned landscape by Robin McKie from The Guardian: http://www.theguardian.com/world/2011/mar/27/chernobyl-disaster-anniversary-japan

Chernobyl twenty years on by Adam Higginbotham in The Observer: http://www.theguardian.com/world/2006/mar/26/nuclear.russia

Chernobyl's Przewalski's horses are poached for meat By Victoria Gill from BBC Nature News: http://www.bbc.co.uk/nature/14277058

Chernobyl's Real Horror Show Isn't the Radiation, It's the Economics by Christopher Mims: http://www.theatlantic.com/technology/archive/2012/05/chernobyls-real-horror-show-isnt-the-radiation-its-the-economics/257842/

Chernobyl's Role in the Fall of the Soviet Union from The Blaze: http://www.theblaze.com/contributions/chernobyls-role-in-the-fall-of-the-soviet-union/

Did Chernobyl Cause the Soviet Union to Explode? from Slate.com: http://www.slate.com/articles/health_and_science/nuclear_power/2013/01/chernobyl_and_the_fall_of_the_soviet_union_gorbachev_s_glasnost_allowed.single.html

Contaminated Regions Resulting from the Chernobyl Accident: http://rusnature.info/env/19_3.htm

Current state of the Red Forest: http://chornobyl.in.ua/en/current-state-red-forest.html

Dispatches from Chernobyl, Part I: Dude, where's your Geiger counter? by Lindsay Fincher from At Home in the Wasteland: http://www.lindsayfincher.com/dispatches-from-chernobyl-part-i-dude-wheres-your-geiger-counter.html

Do Animals in Chernobyl's Fallout Zone Glow? by Mary Mycio at Slate.com: http://www.slate.com/articles/health_and_science/nuclear_power/2013/01/wildlife_in_chernobyl_debate_over_mutations_and_populations_of_plants_and.html

Down with Big Brother: The Fall of the Soviet Empire by Michael Dobbs: http://www.amazon.com/Down-Big-Brother-Soviet-Empire/dp/0679751513/

Effects of the Chernobyl Disaster on Sámi Life by Melanie Blackwell: http://www.utexas.edu/courses/sami/dieda/socio/chernobyl.htm

Elena Filatova's Kidd of Speed, a woman and a hoax: http://www.kiddofspeed.com/chapter1.html and http://www.angelfire.com/extreme4/kiddofspeed/chapter1.html

The End of Ukraine's Balancing Act by Askold Krushelnyckyin Foreign Policy: http://www.foreignpolicy.com/articles/2013/02/06/the_end_of_ukraine_s_balancing_act

The evacuation of Pripyat on YouTube: http://www.youtube.com/watch?v=FrhLueO_Iho&feature=related

Excerpts from the Soviet news conference on Chernobyl from the Associated Press: http://www.apnewsarchive.com/1986/

Excerpts-from-the-Soviet-news-conference-on-Chernobyl-With-AM-Nuclear-Disaster-Bjt/id-0236b2d8853471c57c590ada6ba88975

Frequently Asked Chernobyl Questions from the IAEA: http://www.iaea.org/newscenter/features/chernobyl-15/cherno-faq.shtml

Group wants Fukushima plant preserved for Chernobyl-style tourism: http://ajw.asahi.com/article/0311disaster/fukushima/AJ201302210058

Grumpy Traveler, a review of a Solo East Travel Chernobyl visit: http://www.grumpytraveller.com/articles/chernobyl-tour-review-soloeast-travel-to-pripyat-exclusion-zone-from-kiev-ukraine/

Hanging Out with the Residents of Chernobyl's Exclusion Zone By Ryan Bassil: http://www.vice.com/read/hanging-out-with-the-only-residents-of-chernobyls-exclusion-zone

Heroes of the Hot Zone by Pico Iyer in Vanity Fair: http://www.vanityfair.com/culture/2012/01/japan-201201

Hotel Viru: A Finnish Trojan horse in Soviet Tallinn: http://yle.fi/uutiset/hotel_viru_a_finnish_trojan_horse_in_soviet_tallinn/6501531

How much radiation is too much? A handy guide from PBS.org: http://www.pbs.org/wnet/need-to-know/the-daily-need/how-much-radiation-is-too-much-a-handy-guide/8124/

In Deep Russia, the Camp at the End of the Road by A. M. Rosenthal from the New York Times: http://www.nytimes.com/1988/12/13/opinion/in-deep-russia-the-camp-at-the-end-of-the-road.html

Introduction to radiation: http://www.idahoquad.com/OOPS.html

Is Chernobyl a Wild Kingdom or a radioactive Den of Decay? by Adam Higginbotham: http://www.wired.com/magazine/2011/04/ff_chernobyl/

The Legacy of Chernobyl by Zhores Medvedev: http://www.amazon.com/gp/product/B007N6HW7I/

Life and Fate by Vasily Grossman: http://www.amazon.com/gp/product/B007WL0LFY/

Life in the Chernobyl Zone of Alienation by kuschk: http://basementgeographer.com/life-in-the-chernobyl-zone-of-alienation/

Major biological discovery...inside the Chernobyl reactor? in Doug's Darkworld blog: http://unitedcats.wordpress.com/2007/05/29/major-biological-discoveryinside-the-chernobyl-reactor/

Moscow Hospital Number 6: http://www.nuclearfiles.org/menu/library/media-gallery/image/tredici/102.htm

Mugwort on Wikipedia: http://en.wikipedia.org/wiki/Mugwort

The New Safe Confinement structure on Wikipedia: http://en.wikipedia.org/wiki/New_Safe_Confinement

Novarka: putting a new cap on Chernobyl:http://analysis.nuclearenergyinsider.com/decommissioning/novarka-putting-new-cap-chernobyl

Nuclear Reaction, Why Do Americans Fear Nuclear Power, from PBS's Frontline: http://www.pbs.org/wgbh/pages/frontline/shows/reaction/readings/chernobyl.html

Pripyat photos from Abandoned Kansai: http://abandonedkansai.wordpress.com/2011/02/03/zone-of-alienation-pripyat-middle-school-no-3/

Pripyat.com in English: http://pripyat.com/en

Rad Storm Rising by Gabriel Schoenfeld in The Atlantic Magazine: http://www.theatlantic.com/magazine/archive/1990/12/rad-storm-rising/306380/

Radiation 101: What is it, how much is dangerous, and how does Fukushima compare to Chernobyl? from Blacksmith Institute: http://www.blacksmithinstitute.org/blog/?p=511

Radiation's Complications: Pinning Health Problems on a Nuclear Disaster Isn't So Easy by Charles Q. Choi in Scientific American: http://www.scientificamerican.com/article.cfm?id=pinning-health-problems-nuclear-disaster

The Radioactive Beasts of Chernobyl from Vice.com: http://www.vice.com/the-vice-guide-to-travel/the-radioactive-beasts-of-chernobyl

The Remains of Kursk Submarine from englishrussia.com: http://englishrussia.com/2007/04/16/the-remains-of-kursk-submarine/

Remembering Chernobyl: http://live.huffingtonpost.com/r/segment/chernobyl-anniversary/517a98dc2b8c2a1d5d0003e3

Safety rules at the Chernobylinterinform Agency hotel from MarkR: http://markr.zenfolio.com/p271047341/h2EA46D92#h27b7bf8e

Silent spring by Lauren Monaghan in Cosmos Magazine: http://www.cosmosmagazine.com/features/silent-spring_2/

Solo East Travel, our tour operator for Chernobyl: http://www.ukrainianweb.com/chernobyl_ukraine.htm

Spectre of Kursk haunts Putin from BBC News: http://news.bbc.co.uk/2/hi/europe/1487112.stm

The Truth About Chernobyl Is Told by Zbigniew Jaworowski, M.D., Ph.D., D.Sc.: http://www.21stcenturysciencetech.com/articles/chernobyl.html

Turning Point at Chernobyl by Mikhail Gorbachev at Project Syndicate: http://www.project-syndicate.org/print/turning-point-at-chernobyl

The Twentieth Anniversary of the Chornobyl Nuclear Disaster in Polissia's contaminated north country, village life continues despite health concerns by Alexander B. Kuzma in The Ukrainian Weekly: http://www.ukrweekly.com/old/archive/2006/170617.shtml

Ukraine's president: Chernobyl disaster will cost $180 billion in 2015: http://www.utilityproducts.com/articles/elp-archives/2013/04/ukraine-s-president--chernobyl-disaster-will-cost--180-billion-i.html

Visiting Chernobyl by Ben Lovejoy: http://www.benlovejoy.com/journeys/chernobyl/

Voices from Chernobyl by Svetlana Alexievich: http://www.alexievich.info/knigi/VOICES_FROM_CHERNOBYL.pdf

Wildlife defies Chernobyl radiation By Stephen Mulvey from the BBC: http://news.bbc.co.uk/2/hi/europe/4923342.stm

Wormwood Forest: A Natural History of Chernobyl by Mary Mycio: http://www.amazon.com/gp/product/B004R9Q1LC/

An excerpt from the next book by Bill Murray:

Visiting Easter Island

A Considered Guide for Travelers
What You'll See and What to Know

In the end, you gotta get out of here.

On a bench on the cliffs at Orongo, the center of the Rapanui birdman cult, Marc says the first year was tough. The second, same as the first. He went to Santiago once and, coming from New Zealand, that was culturally absorbing.

Then it got easier. For the last two and a half years, the isolation doesn't intrude anymore. He's got two babies and a Rapanui wife. He thinks she'll be willing to let go of Rapa Nui one of these days but not yet. Marc vows his travel days aren't over, and these days he views the daily flight from South America less as a connection to the wider world than a delivery vehicle for clients.

At 27 degrees south latitude the trade winds blow from the east, so every day at midday the LAN 767 overflies the island at altitude, flies way out beyond it, then turns to descend into the prevailing winds on the NASA-widened air strip. It's the island's only daily interaction with the rest of the world, so you watch.

When yesterday's flight came in we sat at the waterfront watching boys and their surfboards flirt with disaster, in peril of jagged rocks that jut up from the surf. You watch the airplane for the ten minutes, guide it in to land. There's something immediate about that being the only way in and out of here.

NASA elongated the airstrip so that the space shuttle could land here in an emergency. The runway needed 1,420 additional feet to run it out to the 11,055 feet required not just for a shuttle landing, but also for the eventual piggyback retrieval by 747.

Some saw NASA as an imperialist interloper. Some resisted, even derided the scheme.

"The NASA plan is absurd. It's like building a dance floor in the Natural History Museum," said Chilean historian Oscar Pinochet de la Barra, one of the critics of the space shuttle landing project."

In the same June 30, 1985 article the L A Times wrote: "Critics claim the United States will turn the remote island into a strategically placed military base that could drag Chile into the forefront of superpower conflicts and make the country a sitting duck in a nuclear war.

A 1986 L A Times article quoted Rado Miro Pomic, a former Chilean presidential candidate, in an interview in Santiago: "The real purpose of the airport expansion is to enlarge the strategic possibilities in the event of a war with the U.S.S.R. It is logical."

Times were different. The Chilean government that approved extending the runway was a military one, headed by Augusto Pinochet. But for all the angst, as things turned out, nowadays many Rapanui rue the passing of the shuttle program now that Mataveri Airport doesn't reckon on NASA-paid-for runway maintenance.

•••••

The deep mysteries of this island are contested every step of the way, right down to which carbon dating survey is reliable. Some carbon dating points to the area around the only present-day town, Hanga Roa, as one of the first inhabited spots on the island and Tahai is a scant fifteen minute walk from there. To bolster the theory, some suggest the crude features of the Ahu Vai Uri moai prove they were among the earliest moais.

Trying to conjure up the particulars of a civilization's downfall can drive you mad. Tribal violence is plausible to me in a way that wasn't before walking around the island. Seeing one particular defaced (literally, and broken-necked, to press the point) moai out along the road to Tongariki persuaded me it couldn't have been any other way.

There was meanness in the way it was toppled, not just pushed over, but cast to the ground just so, to grind its face into the dirt. To break off its head below the neck.

•••••

Visiting Easter Island, A Considered Guide for Travelers is due in 2014.

ABOUT THE AUTHOR

Bill Murray first ventured outside the United States in 1980. Since then he's traveled to over a hundred countries and territories from Albania to Zimbabwe, mostly with his wife Mirja. They've taken three round-the-world trips.

Bill's first book is ***Common Sense and Whiskey, Modest Adventures Far from Home***, a collection of fifteen stories from Bhutan, Borneo, Burma, Greenland, Guangxi, Lake Baikal, Madagascar, Malawi, Papua New Guinea, Paraguay, Chilean Patagonia, the Southern Caucasus, the Trans-Siberian Railroad, Sri Lanka and Tibet, available in paperback and as an ebook.

Mirja and Bill live on a horse farm in the southern Appalachian mountains of Georgia, USA.

See all the photos in this book and 15,000 more on the author's web site:
www.EarthPhotos.com

Correspond with the author at his travel blog:
www.CommonSenseAndWhiskey.com

Printed in Germany
by Amazon Distribution
GmbH, Leipzig

16980243R00123

If you were eight years old the amusement park may have looked great in 1986, but a kid would flee screaming this morning. Wide, open, windswept and rusted, bumper cars, a gondola ride, a swinging paratrooper-type thing and the iconic ferris wheel stood frozen in time and temperature. The gondolas should have swung in the wind but they were rusted still.

Igor knelt to hold the dosimeter near the ground. 8.65 microSieverts per hour. He brought us here to show us because it was always high right here, on this spot.

"Why?"

Igor the scientist turned up his broad hands.

"Who knows?" His eyes searched ours.

•••••

www.EarthPhotos.com

EarthPhotos Books

ISBN 9780991069705

90000

9 780991 069705